Gary & Jackie
Book #2 Just another Quest
Conscience was written and published
Enjoy
Sheila Bailey M

Life's Awkward Journey

Sheila Bailey Mclaren

Interior graphic arts by
Cassidy Murray
(cassidymurray1997@gmail.com)

My Granddaughter

ISBN 978-1-956896-99-2 (softcover)
ISBN 978-1-957781-00-6 (ebook)

Printed in the United States of America.

Book Vine Press
2516 Highland Dr.
Palatine, IL 60067

This Book is Dedicated to
Kenneth Isaac Bailey
Our Father.

Thank you for the journey ... that is your life.
For the **faith in God** ... that you always followed.
For the **beauty** of your **heart** ... which you continue to use.
For your **individuality** ... not bowing ... to peer pressure.

For the **strength** of your **convictions** ... and following through.
For **courage** ... in the face of **adversity**,
and **perserverance** ... when the road was **less travelled**.

For your creativity ... your genius ... your stubbornness
frustrating ... as that sometimes is!
For the sheer **joy** ... with which you **"embrace your life."**

You have always walked ... tall and proud
yet with a **sweet humility** ... few would understand
you are your own man ... always were ... always will be.

There were the hard times ... the lean times ... the good times,
but at all times ... **we were wrapped safe** ... in the **"arms of love."**

There is no **greater gift** ... than this ... **we are truly blessed**.
Thank you for the **legacy** of a ... **"life well lived."**
May we pass this on to our children ... and they to theirs.

Table of Contents

INSPIRATIONAL / MOTIVATIONAL

The Promise

The darkness fades and a new day dawns.
the miracle of life
and the gift that it is ... is upon us.
I will rush to meet it
and let life unfold ... as it was meant to be.
With hope ... in faith ... I embrace it.
Yesterday is but a memory
of distant possibilities ... unfulilled.
Today the journey continues
and all the possibilities of the world,
they are mine.

Threshold

I STAND AT THE THRESHOLD OF A NEW DAY.
There is only one person standing in my way.
That person is me ... who else could it be?
There are many things that I have felt ... heard ... seen.
There are many places that I have been.
There are memories bitter and sweet
intermixed with each friend I meet.
I am making new memories ... not to replace the old ... but to hold.
I have become strong ... leaving fear behind as I travel along.
For every decision that I make ... for those I must leave behind,
I know that those choices ... are only mine.
I rejoice in the freedom of choice.
With eyes sharpened through the passage of time,
and a clear understanding of ... my heart and mind
I move forward into this new day.
I grow older yet feel not the loss of my youth.
It remains intact within a heart that still believes,
and a mind remembering messages that time leaves.
I am the accumulation of all the love I have known,
the result of every thought and action of my own.
The final story that has yet to be written ... is MINE,
As it has always been since the beginning of time.
There are no excuses that we can find ...
that will unbind us from who we are,
or who we have allowed ourselves ... to become.
There are no excuses ... no ... not one.
I stand at the threshold of a new day ...
I still have time to make the world mine.

The Measure of a Man

There is a standard by which I measure every man I meet.
He stands five foot nine inches ... his hair is snow white.
He weighs in at approximately 160 pounds.
His smile is sweeter than honey ... his heart pure as gold,
his nature ... gentle and sunny.
He is a giver not a taker, how rare.
I have never known him to be the least bit unfair.
sincerity ... honesty ... integrity,
these are the things ... that come naturally to him.
He looks always for good and more times than not,
finds what others ... fail to see.
He is a worker ... a dreamer ... an engineering genius,
shrouded in a cloak of humility,
not prideful about his accomplishments
but rather ... excited by them.
The spirit that motivates him ... in unquenchable,
his faith ... never failing.
He can lift a heavy load in his arms,
as easily as he holds with love ... a small child.
He understands what love is all about ... he is my Dad.
He taught me to believe in myself,
against all odds ... however rough the road.
He taught by example,
tempered always with love ... and complete acceptance.
His strength was unfailing and he never stayed down,
So neither can I.
I want him to be proud of me.
Man can achieve greatness
only when he comes to understand and remember,
all that he has been given.
It is with humility that we accept our imperfections,
And it is with faith ... that we overcome them.
My Dad is the greatest man I know.
He is the standard by which I measure,
every man I meet.
It's hard to compete.

Dream On

Have you ever played the **game of "baseball?"** You win some, you lose some, you tie some and all the while you are out of breath ... you are energized ... you are alive. life is also like that.

I personally love the game and played it often when I was young. I've never lost my hankering for the sheer fun of it. I'm a senior now and I've been advised not to play for reasons of my health. That makes me angry and sometimes anger is good because it is a motivator. Reasons given: my new hip does not allow me to run as I did when I was young. My balance is way off ... like a ship caught in the wind ... I list to the left. My eyes are not 20/20 and glasses are needed to keep me focused.

But ... I'm up at bat. The pitcher is on the mound ... warming up his arm. He is eyeing me up and down, trying to psyche me out. I refuse to be intimidated. I'm holding firmly to my bat ... elbows raised ... knees bent. Will the pitch be slow or fast ... high or low? What about the wicked curve ball? I will not swing until I know!

The ball leaves the pitcher's hand and I pay attention. Whatever is coming I am looking for the **"sweet spot."** The ball is closer now, whistling its way towards the plate. With muscles tense, eyeglasses on straight ... calmly I wait. Timing is everything, **"always in all things."** Ball and bat connect with the sweetest sound. The pitcher comes off the mound as I limp ... quickly towards first base. It's going to be close ... this race. My feet touch the bag. **What a game!** I'm huffing and puffing and my cheeks are red ... but I'm 65 and still going strong. No way that is ever going to be wrong.

I'm never giving up and just so you know ... I expect the same of you! So swing your bat and carry through. Find the **"sweet spot."** Accept no limitations. This **"game of life"** is yours.

Remember ... you are an Army of one setting out to discover ... explore ... overcome ... rejoice in the "victory of you." Do not allow life to pass you by.

You matter ... right here ... right now ... always!

"The Gift"

When you find you are in conflict between your heart and your mind,
and you walk in anger ... with pain not far behind.
When you are stalked by uncertainties ... but driven by pride,
and teardrops fall like raindrops ... and you don't know why,
when pictures in your mind ... disrupt the convictions of your thoughts,
perhaps it is then ... that you should look ... inside your heart.
All things eternal ... begin and never end.
Remember God is waiting ... with a door that opens wide,
and if you will allow it ... he will bring you ... safe inside.
There is but one condition ... by which you must abide,
pain ... jealousy ... anger ... pride,
these must be left ... outside,
for only without them ... can we ourselves ... "survive."
God in his mercy ... taught us to forgive,
and only with **"love"** ... are we worthy to **"walk with him!"**
Always with love.

It's Up To You

If you want to be happy
begin where you are.
Don't wait for some rapture,
that's future and far.
Begin to be joyous,
begin to be glad.
And soon you will forget,
that you were ... "ever sad."

Stepping Stones

With each decision that we make,
another step forward or back we take.
Man is only as great as he believes he can become,
and remains great only when he remembers,
all that he has been given.
Greatness is achieved with,
honesty, integrity and humility,
lest we forget ... **"the stepping stones."**

Onward Ever Onward

Onward ever onward I travel into the great unknown,
trailing with me ... my history from the day I was born.
It all adds up to who I am.
Actions, decisions, steps taken, circumstances, things unforeseen,
all have given me a sense of a self ... I never knew existed.
I am in awe!
I step quietly ... seeking I know not what,
searching out possibilities ... that could be mine
knowing not ... how much time I have to explore.
These things matter ... I am excited!
Like a sleeping flower ... sun kissed ... dew dripped,
I unfurl into this new day.
Looking back over my shoulder ... I see the shadow of a younger me,
innocent ... beautiful ... untouched by tragedy.
Brighter and just behind me,
a strong battle ravaged woman ... pushes me forward,
excitedly whispering **"there is more,"** ... what can she mean?
I turn and smile and wave goodbye ... farewell ... to those days now gone.
Onward ever onward I move forward,
to a future I do not know.
Onward ... ever onward ... I go.

The Gardener's Touch
"Her Children"

Into your hands you were given ...two precious seeds,
to do with ... what you would.
Gently with **infinte care** ... you planted them,
deep in the earths rich dark soil.
You **watched over ... nurtured ... tended,**
and when they sprouted ... you **"rejoiced."**
You **shaped ... pruned ... loved,**
and they grew **strong and straight and true.**
You named the first sweet bud ... for beauty,
and the second strong bud ... for adventure.
They gave ... light .... laughter ... joy,
but most of all ... **"unconditional love."**
The gardener was **touched, and humbled and grateful,**
for the world was ... more precious,
and life itself ... **the ultimate gift.**

Daddy

Your love planted my feet firmly on a path that has led me to here,
an adult grown with children and grandchildren of my own.
The journey was not anything I expected ... nor as beautiful as I wanted.
Like the roller coasters that in later years you made,
my life became a series of ups and downs, with **unexpected twists**.
There was **great joy in simple living** ... and often **tremendous pain**.
I learned that we hurt in direct proportion ... to **our capacity to love**.
I never let go of the knowledge that you instilled in me ... you thought me beautiful.
There is a beauty deep inside that others may not see ... but time cannot erase.
We are the keepers of the hearts ... God gave to us.
To use this gift ... **"is our greatest strength**."
So while living to the fullest ... my **unpredictable life**,
I go forward ... **without fear**.
I search out hearts I meet along the way ... gather them to me,
and here they stay.
These jewels so seldom seen ... so often misunderstood,
are precious **pools of light** ... in a **world going crazy**.
Daddy, thank you for helping me to understand,
the most important ... **"gift from you**,"
is to know ... who I am.

Beginnings Without End

A door closes behind you and locks and you stand alone at the edge of a great void.
You are confused ... cold ... scared ... without hope.
Sadness and sorrow burrow deep in your soul as you recall all that is lost.
Do not lose yourself. The sorrow and sadness, they will pass.
Let the tears fall, feel each drop, let them wash the pain from your heart.
The tracks of your tears are real ... let them work ... let them heal.
When the healing starts, then the miracles happen. **Allow the miracles!**
Now you are standing at the edge of a great adventure and new beginnings.
You taste the fear of the unknown and you feel the excitement of limitless possibilities. Your eyes feast upon the vast repast of natures' bounty, its beauty, buds and blooms.
It bursts forth in a myriad of shapes and colours and scents to entice the pallet.
You partake and are filled with the strength of its goodness.
You have decisions to make, choices. The paths are everywhere,
their destinations ... anywhere.
The only possible stumbling block is you. You step forward with **courage**,
and **Faith** catches you in her arms, and **Hope** takes you by the hand,
leading you into **sunlight**.
It is the sun that guides you steps by day, and at night you **sleep beneath the stars**.
Daily you learn and you grow and you take from the past only memories to treasure, but you never look back. The chains that bound you in pain, lay behind you, **forgotten**, like the broken baubles of a child at play. You are no longer, **that child**.
Actions equal reactions and you realize that you must be responsible for yours,
and that you have no control over the actions of another.
This knowledge sets you free. Your steps quicken and you find you are running,
not away from your life, but rather towards it. You race the wind and you win,
and it's at your back and it's pushing you forward.
Laughter fills the air, and a forgotten something surrounds you.
"It's called JOY!"
You realize that you are happy. You are no longer lost.
Your great adventure led you to **self**.
Live the "**gift of life**" you were given. **Thank God** for the **miracle of you**
and always remember,
endings are only beginnings ... beginnings without end.

Win or Lose

God did not give me wings to fly,
but a soul of my own to reach the sky.
The burdens and sorrows that weigh me down,
helped me search for the strength I've found.
I asked for much and God refused,
teaching me patience ... I can now use.
I have a mind that is not confused,
for always no matter how painful ... I search for truth.
The choices I make are mine to choose,
it's up to me ... if I win or lose.
Will I stretch to the heavens ... or sink to the ground?
Will I see Gods miracles or remain ... Earth bound?
To see myself as I truly am ... to know myself as no one can
is after all ... one of God's greatest ... gift to man.

Simply Said

Humility ... that is what life has taught me,
and a special kind of pride ... few would understand.
I believe in who I am.
I take the good out of the bad and turn it around.
It works beautifully ... I've found.
Giving beyond societies accepted measure,
and building friendships ... that last forever.
Strength is something I have always known,
it allows me to stand without fear ... on my own.
Faith ... in Gods holy plan ... helps me remember always who I am.
Forgiveness comes naturally to me ... for I have always believed,
that goodness exists ... beyond what our eyes can see.
Hate will never be my reality.
I believe in the power of love ... it works for me.
Beyond all pain I have ever known,
rises in beauty ... all the love I have been shown.
Beyond all the riches ... **I do not own**,
are memories to treasure ... that are mine alone.
Beyond all the trials ... that I must face,
lies a powerful ... wonderful ... healing ... faith!
I have all that I will ever need.
Simply said ... I have been blessed indeed.

Breaking Free

I woke up this morning with an idea, a creative thought. I realized that I was no longer lost ... but found. The shattered fragments of my life shifted into place and my concept of self ... was re-established. I was imperfect but learning. I saw beauty of spirit, clarity of mind, heart, courage and unfailing strength and said, "here am I."

I remembered that I was a dreamer, always had been, always would be and I stretched into my old self and I fit, "**like a well-loved glove**." I understood or perhaps remembered in that moment that I was special, that the spark that had ignited my soul at birth was intact. That all the impossibilities were but hurdles to be jumped in a race of:

"life to be won."

My picture of self, had survived the war years. Pain was not a part of that but only a tool by which to learn: that forgiveness was part of healing, necessary to survive. That ultimately we have no enemies except the enemy of self. That there were no restrictions on happiness, except those ... self inflicted. There were no dreams that could not be realized except those we had not the "**courage to dream!**" Hardships were not handicaps but mere stepping stones to "**greater faith**." Beyond ... yet within the stretch of my hands ... is the **gift of self ... God given!**

I am the miracle **"HE" created**. My world will be all that I make it. Humbly I walk, steadily towards **eternity**, amid endless possibilities. The choices ... they are mine!

Challenges

In sweet humility ... knowing our vulnerabilities,
and with a certain knowledge of our strengths,
acknowledging the possibilities of our Dreams,
let us meet lifes' fellow travellers
not as Strangers to be feared,
but rather as souls ... to be reached.
The only impossibilities that we face,
will be in overcoming the misconceptions,
that we ourselves have placed ...
in our hearts and minds.
We can overcome ... anything at all,
If it is TRUTH ... that we wish to find.

Dawn Breaking

My mind was awake before my body was aware that dawn was breaking. I stretched into my day, carefully ... for I am no longer young. I could feel the light fighting against my window blind demanding entry and I checked the time.

I remembered that I had finally fallen asleep and I did it for the first time in a long time ... without the aid of a pill. I call that progress.

The road I travel will be all uphill. My journey must now consist of leaving the darkness ... to walk in the light. This is a choice I make of my own free will but with much sorrow for the hopes that I must leave behind.

I live ... I dream ... I move forward into today. After a long absence I embrace with thankfulness my ... " return to sanity."

Today is a breakthrough ... literally ... with dawns awakening.

Today I take on the full responsibility for the choices ... wrongly made by me. I'm back! I am grateful for that one simple fact.

It does not stop the pain that haunts my days and fills my nights to overflowing. Time alone will heal all the hidden hurting places that no one else can see. Time and a belief once again ... in me.

My search has just begun and spring is all around me. I will search for beauty and for truth. The journey will be taken with faith and courage and wisdom at my side ... keeping me focused on a tomorrow of my ... "own choosing."

The past is GONE and I face a "NEW DAWN!"

It's Rare

It's rare but it's there ... I can feel it, I can heart it, I can see it.
A small group of people come together ... for one common purpose.
With diverse personalities ... talents ... strengths,
but one common bond,
that of dedication ... hard work ... integrity.
Strong ... not by strength of numbers ... but individually,
By sheer strength in their convictions ... in their common beliefs and values.
"In their humanity."
It's rare but it's there ... a small group of people come together,
united by their desire to ... make a difference.
With compassion, integrity, intelligence and truth.
With infinite patience and a sense of the ridiculous,
they go into battle ... fighting indifference, fraud, pain and fear.
Day by day they help ... in tremendous small ways.
They offer hope ... establish direction ... stand up to abuse.
Always they do so ... with "honour."
It shines through... in whatever they do.
A small group of people ... come together,
set apart ...by their excellence!
It's rare ... so very rare ... I see it and I rejoice.

REALITY OF SELF

Interlude

In quiet moments by myself
when no one else intrudes
I clearly see ... who I am.
There is no one there
to whom I must pretend,
no problems to mend.
The picture is much clearer then,
there is just me ... myself ... alone,
with the SOUL that knows me best,
my own!

The Promise

The darkness fades and a new day dawns.
The miracle of life
and the gift that it is ... is upon us.
I will rush to meet it,
and let life unfold ... as it was meant to be.
With hope ... in faith ... I embrace it.
Yesterday is but a memory,
of distant possibilities ... unfulfilled.
Today the journey continues
and all the possibilities of the world
they are mine.

My Reality

I must remember always ... who I am,
and not let life and its tragedies,
destroy the little girl ... that lives within.
The one that still believes ... that love is everything.
I must not lose the innocence of who she was,
while learning through error and heartbreak,
the values ... the world instigates.
I must not sacrifice my pride ... or hide behind lies,
but rather face whatever lies ahead,
with my friend Courage ... at my side.
Wherever I go ... I must follow the conscience of my soul,
knowing that for me ... it's the only way to go.
I must remember I have been given ... eyes with vision clear,
and a mind to explore truth ... far and near,
and a heart that was made ... to listen and to hear.
I have the strength ... within my limbs,
to accomplish ... most anything ... I am blessed indeed.
Now wisdom and patience ... are all I need.
I must keep in perspective ... my goals and objectives,
and not be swayed by the here and now,
for I am searching for a counterpart that fits exactly,
my soul ... my mind ... my heart.
Sweetheart ... I believe I have found him ...in you.
If I am worthy ... you will know that this is true.
Humbly ... with simple pride,
I offer to walk in strength and beauty ... by your side,
to meet lifes' problems ... one by one,
and overcome them all ... with truth, strength, love.
I will not walk behind you ... nor will I rush ahead,
for our footsteps ... must blend.
I will not change in any way ... the man you are,
for love has allowed me to see ... the reality of me.

Choices

Every second ... of every hour ... of every day,
is ours to use or throw away.
Any decisions that we may make,
are our decisions ... make no mistake.
All the trials ... we face each day,
are ours to handle ... in our own way.
None of us can ever really say,
at the closing of another day,
that somebody else ... took our choice away.
The bottom line will always be,
I ... me ... myself ... chose to live my life this way.
The end **result** will always be ... **my responsibility**!

A Stranger Among You

"I love you" ... are words I must not say,
for fear of scaring ... the loved ones away.
How strange!
I must not give too much ... for giving is rare,
and thus is suspect, saying "receiver beware."
How strange!
And if I feel strongly ... anger, love, joy or pain,
I must hold these emotions in reign.
For honesty and openess ... leave no room for,
mystery ... intrigue ... games.
To be accepted ... I must walk carefully,
speak in riddles ... pretend to listen,
smile seldom ... and feel ... hardly at all.
How strange ... how sad ... how strange,
that I am a stranger among you ... for you do not know me!

In All Honesty

You placed the values of a greedy world ... on our relationship,
and thus cheapened it ... those values are not mine,
I told you long ago ... love if not nurtured ...dies.
I do not speak in lies.
There is no monetary standard ... the whole world through,
that can match the priceless gift ... I offered you.
It is a rare commodity ... that cannot be bought
the purity of which ... cannot be measured.
Its beauty transcends ... the artists canvas,
and the poets pen. Its strength ... never ends.
It pays in dividends of ...
understanding ... laughter ... harmony ... peace.
If after balancing the scales ... you wish to be released,
from our investment in each other,
I comply ... I told you long ago,
"love if not nurtured ... dies."
I do not speak in lies.

Insight

The hard questions! If you could, would you undo, erase, even one decision, one action, one mistake, one thought, one word? If you did, how would it ... how could it possibly ... change the direction of your life?

Would that make it better or worse or just different... more challenging? Do you have any regrets or any questions about past actions? Do you sometimes feel lost, ashamed, conflicted, unsure, afraid? Something to think about. We have all been here at one time or the other.

Do you wish you had not been tempted by temptation, whatever it may be and succumbed to it? Should you have been wiser, more strong, less selfish, more giving? Questions are allowed. Seeking answers is a positive action.

Perhaps you should have listened, could have heard more clearly the talk between your heart and your brain. The individual that lives within ... is important.

Have you met self lately? Just asking. Perhaps we all should do a personal check to make sure we are on the right path for us. In all the endless possibilities of our busy lives did we get lost? If so ... is this important to us?

The questions may be hard but the answers are within.

So simple really. Happiness matters ... we matter!

Our life, our choices, our path of discovery, it's all about the journey. You may not want or need to change anything. I'm just suggesting you may want to check in with self occasionally. Remember always that you matter! Truth Matters.

The gift of today is yours. The page is blank, unmarked, ready and waiting for your unique stamp. The choices have always been yours.

Alone

Alone and lonely, it's frightening,
all by myself in a world full of people.
I feel the cold, I hear the silence, I know the emptiness.
There is no direction, no purpose, no meaning,
and I am not special ... in this world full of people.
Time is like a drop of rain, that falls and then disappears,
mixed with the salt of my tears.
Alone and lonely .... it's frightening
all by myself in a world full of people.

The Seasons of my Life

In the spring of my life when every breath was new and sight was clear but confused, I realized that I had arrived as a new born. The world was mine to explore and I had landed in the "land of I Love You." Surrounded by love, handled with love, taught with love. It became the centre of my being. Not knowing anything but love, I took my first steps into this amazing new life, unfettered by anything but joy. What was there to fear? I had no knowledge of fear. No inkling of tears or what would cause them. I had experienced no pain. These were things that I would encounter on the journey I embarked upon and that journey was unplanned.

Step by gentle step I explored the world about me, the people that I met, the beauty of nature that called to me. Bird song and the rustle of the leaves and the gentle wind wrapped around me. Fascinated I stretched into my world. I was safe as I had always been. I walked in faith working on the premise that all those I met would be "similar to me." I trusted. I had no knowledge of greed, jealousy, hunger, anger, desperation or fear. I believed that man was universally good, that hearts were filled with only love, and trust was everywhere. I did not comprehend hate, control, power. I slowly learned that these emotions turned joy into pain. It was a lesson that I wish I did not have to learn.

I kept my illusions for many years, through the summer of my life as I emerged as a teenager. Looking back it was amazing to me that I did not see anything but what was in "the heart of me." I still believed that the world was a beautiful, magical, unlimited place which I could explore.

In the autumn of my life, I fell in love, married and had three beautiful children. They were all miracles to me and through all the days of my life so far, I believed that the world was good. It was misunderstood by some, but it remained pure and sparkling white, unblemished. I had hope.

Somewhere in this season, the colours of my world blended together and became unrecongnizable and my life was filled with pain and despair and I searched for hope and found nothing there. I was unprepared for the finality that nearly totaled me. I realized that I had been wrong about so many things. It was then that I grew up. As I searched for the faith that had always sustained me and reached for the hope that was vital to me, I crawled out from under the pain that was holding me down...and grew strong. What else could I do. While searching for the heart of me...I breathed. I had survived and would bring my family with me.

I was now aware of just how scary life could be. I was prepared. With the best intentions, I soldiered on. In the winter of my life a mind filled with knowledge and the soul of a trooper, holding onto my heart, I stepped stronger than ever into this last stage of my life. I had grown and been taught many lessons and gained wisdom. I was no longer the young girl, carefree and happy. I was a woman grown with children and grandchildren of my own. Each one precious to me.

It has been brought to my attention that perhaps all the years of learning and growth and living have no real meaning to some of those we will soon leave behind. I believe that the young and beautiful, intelligent and strong may tend not to appreciate the wisdom of older and aged and wrinkled and frail and failing. This saddens me and yet I know from experience that each of us must find our own way and make our own paths. It is after all their journey. Remember always "life is a gift."

Self Expression

Self discovery happens when we least expect it. I am constantly learning. I find I am a wee bit Stubborn. There must have always been a defining moment or two where I would enjoy testing the waters, plunging my oar into the river and diverting the natural flow of life ... just a little. A ripple here and a wave there. Here are some examples.

I love clothes, I think they are fun. I put them together in my own particular fashion and strut. The secret of clothes is "**attitude**," take a stride with pride. Be a little ahead of your time.

When I was young I could pull off just about anything. I love the unusual, the unique and just to put a jarring note to a perfect ensemble I would undoubtedly add a weird pair of shoes. "Did you notice me yet?"

Currently the weird running shoes have a practical purpose. They are called orthotics. I get all dressed up to go dancing and add my running to every outfit. Good thing that I started being unorthodox at an early age. Making a statement.

The shoes elicit many comments, some frowns, some smiles from women whose feet are hurting in their stylish heels. Who knows ... I may start a new trend and be a leader for the senior sector.

For example: When I worked at the Public Utilities it was my job to tally up the cash and cheques, roll the coins, (we did that back then) get the deposit ready for the bank and stuff it into an actual bank bag. It looked like a bank bag! Then I would take myself, dressed in high heels (work standards) and smashing outfit out and down the sidewalk two blocks to the bank on the corner.

Looking back on this I wonder why I was not accosted. Anyone could have literally grabbed that bag and run off and I would never have caught them in heels. Into the bank I would go for the daily shuffle, shuffle, taking mincing baby steps up to the teller. In those days you were standing in an unending line of impatient customers. Bored out of my mind and not enjoying the shuffle, I wondered what exactly would happen if I refused to move the next half step. The shuffle started. All those in line ahead of me jumped in to fill the void. I waited.

Those behind me were confused. Their imaginary weight pushed heavily upon my back. I could feel them breathing. I was smiling and wondering what they were thinking. Really, where exactly did they think they were going? They settled back down, but I did not back down and for the fun of it as the line moved once more ... again I stayed. The line behind me leaned in. I was no longer bored. I was pushing the borders of society's acceptance and tolerance for the hell of it, for the fun of it. Inquiring minds want to know ... what if?

HEART BEATS

As Always and Forever

Worn old slippers ... stuffed on tired old feet.
Torn and faded joggers ... hugging the same lean seat.
Hair of a silvery hue ... hangs rumpled, around eyes of blue.
There is still a decided shuffle ... when he walks,
and just a hint of accent ... when he talks.
With glasses perched ... on the end of his nose,
he peers steadily ... towards the door.
I move forward into the light ... and time rolls back.
With arms outstretched ... we reach one for the other,
just two old friends ... reunited and together,
as always ... and forever.

The Journey

The sun rises high into a hot summer sky as the day of departure dawns. A young man no longer a boy moves forward into this day and says his goodbyes and then with purpose he turns and walks away. He is a member of the Canadian Armed Forces and today is the day he leaves, family, friends and homeland.

Another Soldier joins him and another and another as they take their leave of Sweetheart, children, father, mother and friends. This is their very first journey to countries far across the sea, to lands of burning sun and sand and dangers as yet not faced and challenges yet to come.

As strangers in a strange land they come, to stand together, alone, in a place that is not their own. They are far away from all they have ever known. Strong of purpose, clear of mind, honourable, young, healthy and proud. Trained and yet untried under fire. May the fire not come. Who is the enemy and who is friend in a land where war has no beginning and appears to have no end?

God above, please hold these soldiers, close within the protection of your love, in the palm of your hand if you must.

Give them the opportunity to do what they must, come what may. In God and these young soldiers ... we place our love and trust.

My sons best friend came up to me and said, "don't worry ... I've got his back."

Somehow I felt better knowing he was safer.

Once Upon A Wish

I must search for my life and when I find it, I must live it.
I have been granted the rare opportunity to search the ashes of the past,
for an ember still burning with life.
If I find it, I must carry it carefully into the present,
with hope or is it fear?
I need to do this because it is right that I should ... or is it?
This is what I must discover ... one day a long time ago ... we loved one another.
Can this tiny light, with it's puny warmth, be fanned into a flame,
that will bring not one but two ... into the future?
Whether or not this frail foundation ... based on memories of what once were,
and mixed with experiences ... not shared,
will have the strength, the courage, the constancy or even the desire,
to find the truth that now exists ... I do not know.
I only know that I must test this.
I do know that I am scared and confused and a little numb.
That my emotions are chaotic ... and that I am running.
That the memories are beautiful ... yet distorted by a pain I never wish to feel again,
for I am remembering!
Once there were five of us that lived, loved, laughed and trusted together.
There are four that survived and we are heading for home.
I have only two choices ... I must either go back and bring him with me,
or I must step forward, alone, with no regrets for the past I have known.
I must have asked for this opportunity ... for it has been granted me.
I need to see clearly ... I need my friends near me. I ask you to stay.
Gods' will be done in my life ... always I pray.

In The Name Of Friendship

All I ask is that I am ... and might ever be ... your friend.
That I might walk ... beside you proudly,
That I might enjoy the beauty and wisdom of your smile.
That I might kiss you hello ... that I might hug you goodbye.
That I might share with you ... your joy,
and be there ... if you cry.
And when this day is over ... and you and I must part,
I will always ... hold you close ... within the region of my heart.

My Little Flower
(Dedicated to my Daughter)

You are more beautiful than any rose.
I've watched you day by day unfold,
from the precious bundle ... I used to hold,
into the woman child ... I now behold.
I marvel at the strength in you.
You will need that strength ... your whole life through,
and all your newly found ... wisdom too.
The love you hold within ... must be filtered out,
unselfishly ... in day to day living.
All that love will come back someday,
I promise you ... to yourself be true.
I've watched you struggle valiantly ... against all odds,
and rise in sweet perfection ... above the crowd.
You make me proud.
God showers miracles ... on hearts true,
he has one waiting ... just for you.
Always reach for the highest star,
and remember ... who you are.

My Mountain High

I'm standing at the edge of a mountain I've never climbed.
I've left my past and all its sorrow far behind.
The hell that I've been through ... I wonder,
has it prepared me ... for my journey with you?
There is no book of simple safety rules,
the paths before me are mine alone ... to choose.
And my Heaven ... well I found my Heaven ... when I found you.
So take my hand and walk with me. Strengthen and talk to me,
believe ... believe ... believe in the beauty that we see.
My feet are weary and my body aches. I stumble and I make mistakes,
I am humbled and strengthened ... all in one,
for I am reaching to become ... the woman that you love.
There is no compass that directs me. No magic wand to protect me,
yet I will love you ... if you let me, and I will make this mountain mine.
So take my hand and walk with me. Strengthen and talk to me,
believe ... believe ... believe in the truth of you and me.
We stand at the edge of a mountain we've never climbed,
together we will make that mountain ... a Valley in our minds,
snd I will gladly ... walk any Valley left to walk,
with you by my side ... Sweetheart.
The feelings that I am feeling ... they are yours and mine.
The dreams that you are dreaming ... are ours combined.
The love we are sharing ... we will share throughout time.
So take my hand and walk with me ... today ... tomorrow ... and for eternity.
Happiness is ours to achieve ... my darling ... we need only to believe.

Awaiting An Angel

Awaiting an angel ... that would be me.
At first I was but a thought in two hearts.
What would life be ... with the addition of me?
In love I was conceived.
Sent from god above ... I too have been waiting.
Nestled snug beneath my Mommy's heart,
its steady beat ... the music to my sleep.
She is happy ... content in the arms of love.
That would be ... my Daddy.
From a tiny speck to a total me ... I have been growing.
My time is near ... the rhythm is changing.
My journey to you is clear ... are you ready?
The tempo changes ... I am but Seconds away.
Miracle of miracles ... I am yours ... today!

Waves of Tenderness

Thoughts of you wash in waves of tenderness over me.
You have cleansed me of past tragedies.
The pain ... loneliness ... uncertainties,
are but fading memories ... against the memories I share with you.
I must hold true ... to the truth that surrounds you,
as I learn to trust again ... without fear.
In humility and with strength ... I come to you,
stripped of all vanities ... laying naked my soul.
I searched for and found ... a soul mate, a play mate, a heart mate,
and now I search no more.
Thoughts of you wash in waves of tenderness ... over me.
I realize ... I am happy.

It takes a man of vision ... with wisdom ...to find a woman of eternal beauty. It takes a woman of courage and faith to wait for such a man.

Tomorrow

In the beginning I loved you,
for the way you loved my children,
for your humility and your pride,
for your funny and serious side,
for your heart ... that was too big to hide,
for the beauty I felt inside ... when I was with you,
for the patience with our mistakes,
for all the caring ... that love takes.
I loved you then ... a little.
I love you today ... with a love that will not die.
Tomorrow ... I will love you more.
For love survives ... side by side.

Somewhere In Time

As day follows day time has a way of turning,
strangers into friends ... and more.
With each experience shared ... we learned to care,
and are still learning.
Slowly as trust grew ... we let go of some of our fear.
One hand reached for the other,
bonding two hearts that had been hurting, and carefully,
aware of possible pain ... we took a step into a future,
only we together ... could attain. The future is ours to name.
We still have doubts about ourselves perhaps, but not about each other.
There will be misunderstandings ... as we learn this strange language of love,
but we know that the love is there ... we can feel it ... everywhere.
Strength combined with a sweet gentleness,
is what I found in this stranger, who is now my friend.
Under the gruff exterior and clowning around,
is a depth of feeling ... I have seldom found.
My mind told me to fight him ... and I did ... yet my heart allowed him in.
For fleeting moments that first day ... he held my hand.
He has since held my heart ... love grew ... somewhere in time.

Long Way Home

One day upon lifes' road I chanced to meet a soul like mine with the courage to speak. I opened the door and invited him in. I was listening. The story he told was much like my own. Broken hearted he walked alone. I remembered the pain, the sorrow, the confusion, the fear. I opened my arms to draw him near. Gently I wiped away his tears. I remembered all the wasted years I had lost after love had died. Softly I whispered " it's time to heal."

One day I awoke and he was holding me ... so tenderly. He was ready to face lifes' journey once again. Like a flower reaching for the sun ... I marveled at the miracle he had become. My work was done. I was but a stepping stone ... to places unknown. With sorrow I held him one last time this precious soul with a heart like mine. With joy I let him go ... for I knew he had the strength to walk alone. Softly I whispered "goodbye make the world your own."

The days passed and I found that I missed my friend. In the course of my day, my mind strayed. I wondered if I would ever find another soul ... so in tune with mine. Softly I whispered "why did I let him go?" A knock sounded on the door.

He stood there with a foolish grin ... a bunch of flowers and the words "can I come in?" Stunned I stepped aside, holding hope deep inside, hanging onto pride. In wonder he touched my hand and tears of joy, slid down my face. "I missed you" was all he said. "I was lost, confused, afraid to love, afraid to lose." I answered , "I missed you too, I love only you. Your life is yours to choose."

He caught me in a warm embrace ... kisses raining over my face. "I love you too. I do ... you are my miracle ... that is my truth."

NATURES BOUNTY

Ocean's Door

I stood at the edge of the world it seems,
alone under God's Heaven,
and the night came in silently,
the sand shifted beneath my feet,
running to meet the waves retreat,
the breeze was soft and sweet against my cheek,
and the only voice to split the night
came from the pounding on the ocean floor.
Nice and slow again and again and once more.
It was a scene of continuity,
and I sat upon the shore, until the darkness was no more,
and the night was replaced by the miracle of sunlight.
In the warmth of the suns rays, I raised my head in praise,
for within the peace that silenced me,
I could clearly see ... eternity.

The Rythm of the Wind
(From a Walk in the Park)

Wind bent the top of the grasses. It lifted the corners of my jacket. It tugged my hair and was fresh upon my face. The sun ... melted into the day. Peace claimed me.

Dogs barked, squirrels scampered, children ran and parents watched. The wind whirled.

I walked on, under giant trees with branches high. The leaves rustled and the wind danced. Seagulls rose on powerful wings and floated among the currents of the wind, playing ... rising high and falling swiftly. I walked towards the lake and the sun shone on.

Natures natural music of water, waves and wind ... it was like the crash of cymbals in a symphony and it equalled perfect harmony. Natures beauty was displayed before my eyes.

The wind was stronger now as it skimmed and whipped across the surface of the lake. It created waves, sun-kissed like diamonds sparkling ... sprinkled randomly among each crest. They were pushed recklessly towards the rocky shore by the relentless wind, who had control ... crashing like thunder upon the stationary shore. The lake roared!

The waves once united with the rock wall ... raced like a horizontal waterfall across the top and spewed foaming water high into the sun-drenched sky. Wave upon endless wave pounded and crashed against the shore ... orchestrated to the rhythm of the wind.

Beautiful ... powerful ... hypnotic.

Entranced, at peace, humbled, happy, I walked on keeping the lake in sight ... holding me in place against a world ... not always calm.

Night Calling

I stepped into the silence of the night,
the ground lay covered ... in a blanket of pure white.
I paused ... listening to the creek.
It ran swirling ... swiftly ... past my feet.
I raised my eyes searching the sky,
and watched the stars drifting by.
The beauty of the night ... enveloped me.
The world as it truly is ... I see.
My heart filled ... I felt at peace ... I was released.
I have but one life to live ... and so little time.
I have so much yet to give ... to those who are mine.
I must learn to forgive ... so I will be free to live.
The world with its magic ... surrounds me.
I will make it mine ... I still have time.

The Magical Forest

I stepped out of the suns light and into a world of shadow. Silence fell softly upon my head. It lay lightly upon my shoulders. It burrowed deep into my heart. Without sound, I moved forward into the forest. I walked upon a carpet of warm earth dusted with fallen needles and mixed with season's leaves.

The path I followed wandered wide and flowed gently, softly rising then tumbling slowly, hugging the contours up the knolls and down, as if the ground itself ... were breathing. It licked and lapped like ocean waves the border of guardian trees that edged its journey ... pushing, nudging, stubbornly refusing to give way.

Trees like giant sentinels stood proud ... tall ... straight, in row upon cascading row. Their branches swayed and touched and talked to a ... playful breeze that jumped from limb to limb and back again. Trees with breeze ... danced.

Daylight spilled infrequently and without prejudice through tiny openings in God's canopy of trees. It slid down the sides of heavy rippled bark ... filtered through green laced ferns ... sat upon the rotted stumps.

Entranced I continued to walk, lured by the constant and yet ever-changing beauty of this magical forest. I was still in my world but ... the world had stopped moving. It sat hushed and waiting. A few more steps and I would once again be back in chaos. The suns light beckoned.

I wrapped the peace I had found like a cloak about me and stepped with strength ... back into my life. The journey continues ... with hope I embrace it.

Precious Moments

Clouds rippled ... shredded ... stretched,
were stamped upon a sky of palest blue.
The afternoon sun breaking through,
changed the colours from shadowed grey,
to a pristine white hue.
Trees ... leafless ... stark ... cold,
etched stiffened branches into the sky.
The hillside ... gently rising ... lay in a light dusting of snow.
The wind died ... and was lost in the meadow.
Movement on that January afternoon,
was nil ... peaceful ... silent ... still.
Painted by an artists hand ... natures beauty ... stood unheralded,
unplanned ... not noticed.
A picture to be swept away ... within the hours of the day.
Life is constant and yet filled with change,
Like a gift we sometimes ... throw away.
Hold "precious moments" gently in your heart,
to give you strength ... when days are dark.

God's Perfect Canvas

The door swings open slowly upon nature's majesty.
Footsteps land softly upon a walk,
cushioned by fallen seeds.
The grasses ... rain-lashed are spiked ... sharp ... clean.
An early morning sun ... splits through clouds of white,
dispersing the shadows of the night.
A summer breeze stirs high-branched trees,
their foliage full ... cloaked in earth's green.
Souls lift on imaginary wings ... hearts sing.
On God's perfect canvas ... a new day begins.

The Simple Life

I love the dew on the grass ... at the first sign of the day.
I love to walk in tall grass and hear the wind ... swish and sway.
I love the sun on my face ... in the warmth of the day,
and the wind at my back ... pushing me this way and that.

I love the beauty of the lake as ... it's falling asleep,
with the moon shining bright ... and stars filling the night.
I love the smell of logs burning ...under a soft summer sky,
with only God's Heaven ... slowly drifting by.

I love the laughter of children ... and a baby's first Smile,
and the wonder on their faces ... as they embrace life all the while.
I love my childrens sweet faces ... as they lie safe ... asleep in their beds,
and I love God ... in his wisdom ... for blessing me ... with them.
I love you holding my hand, strong and true,
reaping the blessings of two.

Autumn Earth

Defined against the backdrop of a cloud-filled sky,
stands natures' gift of life ... watching the world tumble by.
A sumac bush burning red ... towers over lesser heads,
and is itself overshadowed ... as it pushes against the pines,
that line the creek bed.
Raindrops ... falling faster ... race with leaves spiralling down,
joining other odd-shaped friends
who have already touched the ground.
Crisp, crunch, burnt and bent
leaves meet raindrops ... and blend.
At earths surface ... their journey ends.
Night delights ... in daylight's early flight.
Stars hang low ... in Autumn's glow.
Chill winds nip sweet-scented air
peace and beauty are everywhere.
I wish to walk through the seasons of my life,
with friends ... will you be there at the end?

Clouds

They can be pretty ... can't they?
On a brisk evening in the fall ... when the sun is just setting,
and the sky turns a bright orange,
and you stop to appreciate how beautiful it is,
or that day that you ... sat on your lawn,
and watched the sky.
So much time that you spent with him,
that you swore you would ... "**never forget**."
You know that the day passed ... before we even thought about it.
But time ... didn't matter then,
all that mattered was that we ... **loved each other**,
and we could see how beautiful our world ... really is.
It's not often we stop to think ... about the little things.
Like the barista who gave you a genuine smile ... at the coffee shop.
Or the sweet old lady near your house.
We rarely appreciate, how much those small things mean to us,
and he was the one who helped ... you see that.
He was your hero ... in a sense.
When the clouds consumed you ... and everything seemed great,
he came in with his beautiful colours and showed you what ... life meant.
He showed you that there's more ... than just ... "greyscale."
He introduced you to ... "the rainbow."
He is the one who opened your eyes to ... "the sunset."
And the pretty colours the leaves changed into ... in the fall.
He was the one who showed you ... "**what life is.**"

Given to me by my beautiful grandaughter: Alyssa Principe McLaren

TO MOVE BEYOND LOSS

Eternal Journey

We have climbed mountains high,
sheltered in valleys low.
At jouneys end ... together once more,
hand in hand ... we walk ... through "Heavens Door."

Mother

I WONDER: Did I take for granted my mother's endless love,
the burdens that she carried, the worry, trouble, tragedy,
Within the "heart of family."
The countless, endless, giving ... that she gave,
the sacrifices that she made, of hopes and dreams,
that she let fade.
Why: So she could be the mother ... that I need.

I WONDER: Do I take as my "just reward,"
the arms so warm ... that hug and hold.
The hands grown worn that cook, clean, toil.
The voice that changes ... that praises ... that scolds.
Her eyes ... tired now ... saw past,
dirt, grime and countless crimes,
to the "**potential of the child inside**."

I WONDER: Did I take as my right ... without a thought,
the hopes and dreams that ... she forgot.
Why: So she could be ... the mother that I need.
With all my heart ... I thank you true.
"dearest mother ... I love you."

To Walk in Faith

I must let go of all this pain and sorrow.
I must look ahead to a new tomorrow.
I must have patience to allow ... what I deserve to happen now.
I must not question the how or the why,
but trust in God to hear my cry.
To walk in faith ... I must fight the despair that is everywhere,
and find the strength to put hope there.
I must remember all I have been given, and all the love I knew.
I must trust in God ... to see me through.
To walk in faith I must walk away from you,
even if it feels ... wrong that I do.
I must allow God in his wisdom ... to do what is right for you.
Only a miracle of love ... will undo this senseless thing you do.
And bring us back to the love we knew.
If tomorrow for us never comes ... I will know that Gods will is done.
I will walk in faith ... may God always walk with you.

The Next Step

The snow fell softly all that day ... mixed with sunlight.
It continued to fall steadily ... through the night.
A blanket of white spread across the fields and hills,
caught on tree branches bare ... swirled in breezes ... filled the air.
The roads were thick with it ... beautiful ... unmarked ... pure.
The world grew quiet ... muted ... peaceful ... still.
And into this place ... and this night,
God came quietly ... reached out his hands,
gathered her gently ... in loving arms ... and carried her home.
We thought we were too late ... but the secret of love is ... it waits.
There are countless stars that shine on high,
and other worlds ... beyond our eyes.
But here on earth ... we live by faith ... searching for truth.
Always there are those ... God has set apart.
They walk with strength ... courage ... and purity of heart.
They put their hand in the hand of God ... holding firm to the iron rod.
They are the soldiers ... that walk ... unchallenged ... humbly ... unto glory.
Mom ... you are one of them ... we will meet again at my next step.

Legacy of a Simple Man

We never wanted to say goodbye dad ... we never wanted to see you suffer,
yet through it all you showed to us that mind over matter ... matters.
Hearts will always lead to truth and faith will carry you safely to forever.
Your journey continues and yet we, your family,
know that love continues to grow if you want it to.
When hearts meet with complete understanding
and sometimes needed forgiveness,
there is no force more powerful.
That kind of power when used for good ...
is the power which should move our world.
Each one of us in our own unique way ... can make a difference.
You taught us that... and you never looked back.
You probably thought we would just follow through.
Dad you did make a difference, without criticism, without judgement.
With simple acceptance, love and approval ... you lifted us up.
You are a hard act to follow but we believe that your family is up to the challenge.
You always dreamed huge dreams with no doubts or restrictions,
on what you could accomplish.
You were a force to be reckoned with.
You were never aware ... of that simple fact.
We saw it and we believed ... like a beacon in a storm-tossed night,
your gentle, unfailing light carved the path ... that we should follow.
You left us a legacy worth far more than all the world's gold.
Love unlimited is what you gave ... nothing and nobody can ever take that away.
Your family is richer by far ... than you can ever imagine.
With love you taught us to believe in who we are ... that is so amazing!
You will always be the light ... we choose to follow.

Morgan Douglas/Kaleb Kevin

On your journey to our world, a place called earth, suddenly you both changed course. For reasons we do not know or as yet cannot understand, while we were dreaming babies ... God in his wisdom had other plans. One moment you were coming straight to us and then were turned around. You were "**heaven bound**." You left us feeling lost, bereft, alone ... our hearts hurting, for the possibility of you and all the joy you would bring, was changed instantly to ... only the wonder of what might have been.

We held you for mere **fragments of time** in the **PALM OF OUR HANDS**. So tiny, so delicate, so perfectly formed ... and in those few moments we knew ... the miracle of each of you.

Heavenly father called you home to a placed of harmony and peace and ultimate joy. He holds you close and he keeps you warm and safe. This is your "**sweet destiny**." Now your voices will blend with the **angels** and you will play together ... among the stars. If we look we will see you twinkling a little brighter than the others and know ... that you are ours! We may see you jumping on puffy clouds, soft, thick and white, scattering pictures across our sky, or **flying** on the **wings of eagles in flight**. You may fall asleep within the blanket that we know ... **as night**.

You can slip into our world on the **rays of a sunbeam** or be the brightest flower in the garden and you can play and romp in the **thunder of the surf** ... leaving your footprints in the sand for us to follow. If we listen we will hear you **whisper in the wind**, your music the rushing creek and the crackling leaves.

You have opened our eyes to the **beauty of the miracles** that surround us. You will be within each miracle that we find. We will keep searching for miracles until once again ... we can be with you. Keep busy our **little angels**, using **heavenly strokes** to colour our world so never again will we fail to see the magic ... the beauty ... the **mystery of life's infinite possibilities**.

On the rare days you find us stumbling on the roads, down below, jumbled in our mind with hearts a little sore ... slip in once again at the end of a rainbow. Be the calm after the storm ... the wind kissing our brow ... the sunshine opening our eyes to the **miracle ... that is "our life."**

We have gained a greater knowledge of creation and a clearer understanding that **life itself** is a **gift** each one of us must treasure. Forever we will try to remember ... what we have learned.

Morgan Douglas and Kaleb Kevin ... know always that you are loved.
- Grandma

Lady
(Dedicated to: Nina Cattafi)

She walks with grace beneath a weight of responsibility,
a gentle soul ... carrying a beautiful heart.
She is forever giving of self and bending to the will of others,
yet her strength ... will not allow her to falter.
As a wife, mother, grandmother ... she is unmatched ... or so it seems.
Selflessness ... is a code she lives by.
Love is what she gives ... all she needs.
She is intelligent, wise, fun, creative, young at heart.
Her natural talents ... limitless.
Her frailty ... masks an indomitable spirit.
She owns her own soul.
This lady ... for such is she,
is deserving of all the joy ... her heart can hold,
and ultimate joy ... will be her reward.
We do reap ... that which we sow.
Her garden is flourishing ... in the house of the Lord.
I do know and have always loved ... who you are.

Mom

Heavenly Father must have known that I needed you for my mom. I am grateful to have been chosen to be one of your daughters. I knew you were not there in that hospital room. I could not feel your essence. You had gone on to the next step of your journey.

The snow fell softly all that day, mixed with sunlight. It continued to fall steadily as we drove through the night. A blanket of white spread across the fields and hills, caught on tree branches bare, swirled in breezes, filled the air. The roads were thick with it, beautiful, unmarked, pure.

The world grew quiet, muted, peaceful, still, **and into this place and this night ... God** came quietly, reached out **his hands**, gathered you gently in loving arms and carried you safely home. You needed to go. We thought we were too late ... but the secret of love is ... **"it waits."**

I know mom is waiting for us now and **"fear not,"** mom will still be directing our footsteps here below, from up above. In countless ways when we need to make choices ... hers will be the voice we hear. Around ever corner, memories will come. **They equal love**. A clear running stream backed by Sumac will remind us of home. Roast beef done to perfection and strawberry rhubarb pie. Mom at the end of a broom chasing racoons off the balcony and placing muffins on the clothesline for the squirrels. I will be watching more baseball games because she loved them. She was like chinese food ... both sweet and sour, the combination ... **IRRESTIBLE**.

I am looking at the faces of your family mom. Starting with dad, your children, your grandchildren and great grandchildren. They are beautiful mom, **individual, unique, precious**. Into each life you have, stretched their minds, opened their hearts, shown them strength, pushed them to follow their own dreams, shaped and molded. This may not be the picture that you could have painted, if given the time, but they are "**your masterpiece mom, your lifes work**." Well done. You could have given me no greater GIFT, than this family.

There are countless stars that shine on high and other worlds, beyond our eyes ... but here on earth we live by faith and search for truth. Always there are those that **GOD has set apart**. They walk with strength, courage and purity of heart. They put their hand in the "**Hand of God," holding firm to the iron rod**." They are the soldiers which walk, **unchallenged, humbly, unto glory**.

Mom: you are one of them!

My mom was a January 1st baby along with her older sister. They are both gone now. Mom departed January 6, 2011 and we her children can no longer celebrate her birth, we can however remember her life and the gift of sacrifice and love that she always gave to us.

Grandmothers

The Lord made and gave to us all things great and small,
but the best of his work is found in grandmothers,
who are mothers ... one and all. Here for always ... always in our hearts.
They have lived and loved ... laughed and cried ... before us,
they have sown the seeds, with which to feed us,
nurtured, loved, listened to and forgave us.
Grandmothers are somehow special. They are those “God” set apart,
to lead us and to guide us ... with a tender and loving heart.
With arms to comfort and a listening ear,
hearing that which others fail to hear.
They watch us with eyes wise enough to see,
where our footsteps, youth and inexperience leads.
Seeing our goodness ... past all our faults,
with eyes that know us only ... from the region of their hearts.
They have the wisdom of their years, knowing all things, our hopes our fears.
They have walked the roads that we approach ... offering us a “world of hope.”

Grandfathers

Grandfathers sentiments are seldom heard,
they speak by action ... not by word
those big hearts they try to hide,
result in hugs and pride filled eyes.
A gruff voice cheers us on,
a hearty roar tells us ... when we're wrong.
All these things let us know ... that we belong.
Grandfather, who has given so much,
and has so much more to give,
let us learn from your example,
and sample what life has to give.
Like yours ... may our spirit be,
always strong and sure,
knowing that the right decision ... is always pure.
May we grow in strength and in wisdom,
as you have taught us to,
and enjoy the fruits of giving ... as shown by you.
May we be deserving ... of the grandfather that is you.
Grandfathers are somehow special,
they are those ... that God has set apart.

In Memory: J.C.M.
(April 2021)

A soul has flown this earthly coil,
freed from earth bound cares.
We shall not meet again, my friend,
not here my friend,
only within the region I hold dear.
Memories of one now gone, yet not forgotten.
You brought me no pain ... no tears,
only hope given down through the years.
Peace and a time to reflect.
Happiness and a world of possibilities,
that I could not reject.
A safe place ... a laugh ... a kiss,
hope and strength.
All things made new again,
through knowing you.
Your heart ... your mind ... your soul.
I was a friend in need.
You were a friend indeed.
You are not forgotten.
You reside safe inside,
a heart once broken ... now whole.
A gentle reminder of goodness,
that the world ... did not spoil.

(With sorrow and hope to those that you love.)

ARE WE STUCK?

Sorrow No More

Let it go ... just let love go.
Let it drift behind you.
As each new path appears ... say goodbye,
to tears that never dry.
Take the time to heal ... try.
Let love go ... just let love go.
Let it blow off the edge of the storm.
Let pain fade and hide your face no more.
Smile and soon your heart will know,
that it has wings on which to soar.
Let love go ... and sorrow no more.
If love hurts ... and sadness rules your days,
and tears are never far away,
the love is wrong ... walk away ... be strong.
Save your heart for a heart that cares.
Reach within ... dig deep ... win.
Let love go ... just let it go.
And sorrow ... sorrow no more.

My Fatherless Son
(My Window View)

A young boy with dark tousled curls framing a sweet little face, wanders aimlessly on the stone slab patio of his **borrowed home**. The sun is shining and the background of dense trees running down to surround the creek make his playground a haven for most little boys, yet there is no sunshine in his eyes and his mouth refuses a smile. His young frame, football broad is gangly now as he stretches to fill his advanced age. Eleven is all.

The basketball that fills his child's hands, bounces periodically up and down, but he does not try for a basket. Perhaps he does not believe that he can. He does not believe in anything and there is little heart left. Shoulders slumped, head down, there is no Confidence in his step. No joy. He comes once again to the door and asks if "J" has called. "No" I said. "Right" says he trying to be strong, and shrugging his tiny shoulders he walks away. A tear runs down his cheek and disappears in the fist of his hand. I watch, heart breaking and helpless to help. I ask myself the age old question, "**why?**"

My son, mostly fatherless since eight, had found a friend, a best friend, almost a dad. This man had played with him and worked with him and loved him every single day. He had chased the shadows away and brought **laughter and joy** to this one small boy. I guess it was too much to ask of any man that he continue to see my son. It was too much to hope for that this stranger who had become a friend would allow a friendship of such importance, not to end.

Isn't life strange ... strange and cruel that one so small should walk without hope, without joy. I was only a mom and I could not fill this void.

It has been my observation that some men are just little boys, playing with their toys, there for the good times, unable to find the strength for the hard. They profess to know what love is, but it's just a whim and no one really wins. They forget what truth is, if they ever knew. When the sun is shining ... they shine and with the rain ... they run.

The stranger that became our friend, sadly was one of them. I thought he was different. I was wrong. I believed in him. It was wrong that I did. I trusted him and he left only pain. My love and assurance will not change the sadness in my little boys heart, but he is a survivor just like his mom and he will be fair and strong and make me proud.

God is love ... the ultimate love we can believe in. We will believe ... in the name of love.

Dream Lover

Dark lashes shadowed pale cheeks as she lay ... peaceful in sleep. Like a kitten she snuggled deeper, backing up to the warmth of him. Her head tucked naturally under his chin, her legs tangled with the familiar weight of his. Cradled within the safety of two strong arms ... she dreamed.

A sweet smile gently lifted the corners of her lips. She turned burrowing into his chest and slowly she awakened ... running tiny hands softly against the contours and textures she knew so well. Her fingers slid through the curled hairs and tugged playfully. He pulled her closer ... as on he slept.

Her hands continued their travels, twining with his ... moving slowly up muscled arms, across broad shoulders and then tracing, delicately, the outlines of his beloved face. The high brow, the prominent nose ... a little broken, the full often pouting lips ... always demanding. His beautiful eyes so wonderfully brown, so warm, so deep ... were hidden now in sleep.

Holding his face she barley touched her lips to his ... quietly whispering, "I love you." The man was awake ... had been for some time. In one swift movement she was swept under him. He was everywhere, his lips taking ... drinking deeply. Strong hands tenderly cupped the fullness of her breasts ... the nipples hardening against the palms of his hands. Like liquid gold their bodies melted into one fluid motion ... a symphony of perfect harmony ... the song one of love. It was always like this ... a touch, a look, a question, an answer... peace!

In need she reached for him. There was nobody there. It had been but another dream and now she was awake ... her eyes confused by the darkness. Her pillow was damp with the tears that had carried her, exhausted ... to forgetfulness in sleep. How long had his absence been, hours, days, months?

It seemed there was no end to the pain. Memories always memories without end.

An Opportunity for Change

A blank piece of paper with no words left to write.
A life in turmoil ... no answer right.
A heart in pieces ... beyond repair,
faith wavering ... no answer there.
Courage turned to despair ... a lost soul wanders there.
Truth becomes a matter of conjecture ... changed by a point of view,
but whose?
We try ... we win ... we fail ... we lose,
choices matter ... I'm confused.
Memories of yesterday ... its warmth, its light,
contradict todays plight.
If nobody is wrong ... name the enemy we fight.
Too many variables make up the pattern of our lives.
We fought the battles, carried the pain ... and now wear the scars.
Too many mistakes made ... to change the outcome after all.
We win ... we lose ... we try ... we fail.
Is there anyone left who cares?
I hear the world awakening beyond my window-pane.
A new day dawns ... the nightmare fades.
Today ... is an opportunity for change!

"Why"

Why do we do the things that we do,
or say the things that we say?
Why do we follow only familiar paths,
is it because we know the way.
Why can't we go forward ... without looking back?
Why can't we let go ... of something or someone,
who is leading us ... off track?
Why must we always harbour fear,
and labour in despair?
Why must we always ... choose not to see,
when the truth we seek ... is there?
Why are we afraid to feel ... to give ... to care?
Why must we go with the ... life that we know,
and leave the future ... untried,
like a present under the tree ... still wrapped and tied?
Why are we afraid to love ... when the gift of love ... is so rare?
Why ... I ask why ... do I care?

Undiagnosed Insanity

It's a rare disease not easily detected,
the patient appearing normal ... waking, talking, working, playing.
It is only when he draws near and interacts and then reacts,
that the symptoms appear and the confusion begins,
for it is then ... that he walks with fear.
He appears confident, strong, sure ... his intellect is superb,
yet he is insecure and his understanding nil,
for he does not know ... what truth is.
The cause is trauma and pain so severe ... it severs the connections forever,
from heart to soul to brain ... and the patient is never quite the same.
The candidates for undiagnosed insanity ... are from the crème of the crop,
the very top of humanity ... those who once had hearts,
and someone, somewhere ... made those poor hearts bleed,
leaving them ... alone in dire need.
They are the faithful and the true, those that trusted and had compassion,
and someone, somewhere, broke that sacred trust,
to feed their own selfishness.
Trust turned to distrust and compassion disappeared,
and the patient himself, sat in judgement upon all those who appeared,
after the pain.
Forgiveness was not something that came easily or even at all,
and all the love and care ... once so freely given,
was driven underground ... till there was nothing there.
Those that cared were frozen out ... by this poor broken heart,
that time did not repair.
To love them only causes pain ... and yet they must have love,
their life to sustain.
The tragedy is ... that they cannot live with reality,
and that my friend ... is the definition of this malady.
The only cure is love ... and that is the one thing,
they can no longer believe in.
In vain we try to reach ... those that we love.

Blue Christmas

Head bent, shoulders hunched ... feet tangled like his thoughts,
he remembers the people he cared about,
the life they shared ... the growing together and drifting apart,
the joys and tragedies ... all are memories.
Quietly he assesses who he is ... what he has achieved,
and what he now believes ... can make him happy.
He is healthy, handsome, strong ... what went wrong?
A tiny tree stands unbalanced by the window,
overshadowed by a giant red stocking, dangling ... dangerously,
from the fireplace.
This effort for Christmas ... is not his.
Two young laughing children ... try to make this house a home.
They surround him with the only real love ... he has allowed or known.
Night steals in through the windows ... placing shadows about the room,
matching the shadows ... hidden in his heart.
A single tear ... not noticed ... accents the lines of his face,
leaving not a trace ... of the torment within.
He shivers ... feeling the cold.
He is all alone and having ... "**a blue Christmas**."

Broken Dreams

Down the road of broken dreams,
I walk alone remembering.
My vision of the past is very clear.
My fears about tomorrow ... more than real.
I am more tired that I have ever been.
Sometimes too tired to try again.

The smile pasted upon my face,
does not reflect my inner space.
Sadness reigns forever there,
my soul in pain ... laid bare.
My faith in those I once loved ... gone.

Everywhere I look ... the picture's wrong.
As down the road of broken dreams,
I walk ... alone ... remembering.

Unravelling

I am unravelling the chords of love around my heart,
note by note, string by string ... are you listening?
I'm letting go ... I set you free ... for you are not in love with me.
The love that binds your heart to mine ... did not come from you,
I but wanted it to ... the dream was mine, not yours,
I'm letting go ... I set you free ... to follow your own dreams.
Step by step ... inch by inch ... I'm moving away from you,
because you asked me to ... because I'm in love with you.
No longer am I confused ... it's only right that I do this ... for you.
Tomorrow when you wake ... I will be gone,
But a memory of things gone wrong ... only a fragment ... part of a song,
echoes of a love ... that did not belong.
I'm unravelling the chords of love that bind ... your life to mine.
The heart strings... one by one have come undone.
With love I set you free ... to be happy ... in a world without me.
Only love remains ... yours unclaimed ... without chains.
I sacrificed my heart for you ... my heart holds true,
for I found you worthy ... of the love you refused.
Are you listening ... love is whispering,
can you hear it ... tapping gently against your heart?
Be happy Sweetheart.

Hidden Treasures

If you look and do not see,
touch and do not feel,
listen and do not hear,
perhaps you are lost.
Treasures can be discovered,
in out of the way places,
or just around the next corner.
Be prepared to uncover,
all that you discover,
and it will ... enhance your life
take a chance.

FLOUNDERING INTO PERSPECTIVE

Andy

Little scamp, spoiled brat, little boy blue. You choose. His name was Andy and he was all of three. His head was turned towards the sitter who sat beside him in the booth. The restaurant was busy over the lunch hour but before me a real-life drama was being enacted. I did not want to be there. It was and stayed ... a battle of wills ... and I was an unwilling participant, but it was not my will that came into play.

I watched from across the table, one little boy and one determined sitter. She had just told him to look at her and he had. So close I could have touched him had I reached across the table that separated us. So close and yet so far. I saw clearly the sweet line of his plump firm cheek, his determined little chin, the downward curve of his full rosy lips. I sat spellbound as the sweep of thick lashes were raised to reveal the most beautiful blue eyes. These eyes were trained, unflinchingly ... upon the face of his sitter. He was stubborn yes, that could not be denied but I wondered in this instance why? It was such a simple thing she asked of him that created an obstacle too large to squash.

His small head was held proud ... upon little shoulders bowed ... beneath the weight of her censure. He was not going to say "please." No matter the pressure she inflicted and that was great, he stood his ground against the harsh words that battered around his head. It was but conjecture on my part, only a feeling within my heart, that his wee heart was hurting, broken. The eyes held all his thoughts, silently pleading that she would relent. His fisted hands sat still upon the table, never moving. He did not squirm, not once in his seat, nor did he kick his little feet under the table. I would have known. The only movement that I saw at all, were the convulsive workings of his throat as he fought valiantly to keep back the tears that glistened and threatened to drop. I watched helpless as he overcame the need to cry. So little, so young, so determined. He would not back down. He would not say "please."

He was only three, what could we do? He was only a baby still and I so much wanted to gather him safely to me and hold him tight. I wished with all my heart to place a smile upon that dear sweet mouth. I wanted to tell him it didn't matter, that he did not have to say "please" and pour that ketchup over his chips. Time after time, bypassing the sitter, I tried to humour, cajole, tempt, play and practice my please and thanks, all to no avail. I could not save him. He would not be saved. Then when I least expected it I heard a small voice say quietly ... "please."

That was all I needed. Quickly I ripped open the packet of ketchup and dumped it down by his fries. He looked at me with a sparkle in his eyes. Short stubby fingers picked up the fry and dipped and dove it into his mouth. Andy shyly offered one of those prized fries to me. The hell with my diet. I said, "thank you Andy." He just looked at me and gave me another. We had no more trouble, but I'm still troubled. What was all that stubbornness about? Why dig in his heels when he could have dug in his fingers? There is only one thing for certain. The little boy blue, a baby still, was pulling his own strings. He was living his own story. He was fighting his own battles and winning, however imaginary these battles might have been ... they were very real to him. He made me a believer in the strength of the human soul. From one so young to one so old.

Rear View

I took my kids to school today and driving home I passed,
another group of kids ... playing in the grass.
One little boy detached himself from the crowd,
walking towards the road.
I slowed down ... but he did not cross.
He laid his school bag down and dropped to the ground.
Drawing his knees up under his chin,
his arms went around them to hold them in.
He lowered his head and started to cry.
I don't know why.
I watched him in my rear-view mirror.
I had no right to interfere.
I will wonder about that little boy all day long.
I will wonder where he's gone.
I will wonder if I was wrong ... to stand clear.
The last time I saw him,
he was crying ... in my rear-view mirror.

(This was me not getting involved ... I wonder how often this happens.)

Stay or Go

I ask myself day and night ... night and day,
should I go ... or should I stay?
Always ... love gets in my way.
If I choose to walk away ... I lose.
If I stay as it is today ... I've already lost.
How great is the cost?
Is it better to remain with you ... in pain,
or stand all alone ... once again?
Do I value myself ... not at all?
Is this then ... the reason I stall?
For surely it is a stranger ... that keeps hurting me,
or a blind man ... refusing to see.
I must choose my reality,
to stay with you ... or be happy.
Yesterday can be but a memory.
Tomorrow a tragedy.
Today I live and die ... by my choice.
I must decide.

Broken

Little lady, crazy baby or broken doll.
Rules, ethics, morals, do they mean ... anything at all?
The pallet lays smeared with life's muck,
the artists' hand is frozen ... stuck,
inspiration stayed, the picture unfinished,
its clarity frayed.
Upon the canvas the face is plain, etched in pain.
Drops of tears, stop sharply on the unfinished page.
The eyes are confused ... hurt ... dim,
like a candle whose light is fading, from fighting the storms within.
Her grasp on reality is tunnelled to this time, this place.
She dangles at the top of the world ... holding tight,
with two tiny hands, the knuckles ... stark ... white,
grasping an axel, rusted and cracked,
swaying earth-bound and swinging back.
Her body floats ... weightless ... in fathomless space.
There is no time ... has she run her last race?
Soft lips tremble, upon silent screams ... that go on forever.
Like a broken doll, beyond recall ... she awaits the end.
Her last prayer ... to feel ... nothing at all.
A little lady, crazy baby or broken doll.
The picture is incomplete ... yet the picture says it all.

Remembering

I remember in the beginning ... the awareness.
The reaching out ... the searching for,
the wonder of discovering ... more and more and more.
There were just us two ... moments together were moments too few.
We never lacked for things to say ... we seemed to compliment each other,
In the most extraordinary way.
The harmony of heart and mind that we uncovered,
left a wealth of joy and happiness to be discovered.
Do you remember?
I remember in the beginning ... we spoke the same language and were understood.
We laughed together and it felt right and good.
The silences were precious time ... where thoughts and feelings intertwined.
I remember the dreams we dreamed together,
I thought they would go on forever.
Do you remember?
I was wrong it seems about so many things.
I remember in the beginning ... when I thought I loved you.
I remember when I knew I loved you.
I remember wishing I didn't Love you.
Do you remember?
Isn't it strange how we sometimes allow,
life as we comprehend it ... to interfere with happiness?
Strange but not funny and I am not laughing now.

Dare to Dream

Goodmorning. I hope you are still travelling with me on this bumpy winding road. Are your shocks in good repair? Today is all about living the life you have been given and making it yours. Life is a circle of continuity. It will not be thwarted. Rather life must be engaged. You must taste it, feel it, conquer it. It's a hell of a ride and its yours to command. Something to think about.

If I could I would, give you the world, but it is not mine to give. The world and all that it has in store for you, is yours already. Do not stand on the sidelines. Life is the pallet, you are the artist! Do not hesitate or all could be lost. Begin to paint. Paint in large, bold strokes with all the colour there is to see. Be creative, be imaginative, be strong and take chances. Do not be left behind in the dust of the world's participants. Shout out loud if you have to and believe, "this world is mine!"

Capture the sunsets over a crystal-clear lake. It's beautiful. Mirror the mountains into it. Catch the evergreens towering along the shore. Grab a seagull flying high and place it in your sky. Remember this picture is yours! A baby round and rosy playing in the sand and a lonely old man with a fishing rod in his hand, these can be factored in. a faded rowboat bobbing in the bay, a log cabin sitting on a jut of rocks, wet footprints on the dock, take note of these. Look ... see ...believe.

Remember that treasures can be discovered in out-of-the-way places or just around the next corner. Dare to dream.

Do not miss a single one of the miracles that come your way. Today is your day ... always into infinity, if only you want it to be.

The Happy Homemaker

There was singing about the house and racing steps,
and story books taken off the shelf,
to be listened to with delight.
There were toys strewn about the room,
and at times even underfoot,
but the floors were vacuumed, the beds all made,
and lots of home cooked food.
The two budgie birds gazed on the happy confusion,
adding their voices to the laughter in the air,
and everywhere ... there was LOVE.
A stranger looking in would see,
but three making all the noise within.
A father with rumpled hair of silver threads,
and two dark, unruly heads.
Upon the couch they sat,
the youngest a little girl snuggled on her daddy's lap.
His son curled within the haven of his arm.
Here they sat at close of day ... intact,
the happy homemaker ... with his cherished pack.

The Door

I close the door softly behind me,
on the life I knew before.
I cannot go there anymore.
The time has come to say goodbye.
To leave behind tears ... that have dried.
To forget promises made ... but not fulfilled.
To treasure the beauty ... that I remember still.
The door clicks smoothly into its space,
and I know that I must leave this place.
There is no peace here ... nor will there ever be.
The gift of love we shared ... is beyond repair.
I wish it were not so ... but I can sorrow ... no more,
and we stopped believing in us ... long ago.
The door stands a silent testament ... of what we cannot forget.
Immovable as our stubbornness and useless pride,
as strong as our anger ... as deep as our pain,
can something called love ... remain?
Forgive me for not believing ... in you.
Accept that for me ... your actions ... equalled our truth.

Midnight Caller

Fingers dial my number at random one by one. The phone rings and I answer.
"Hello," I say and the music starts to play. The time is 12:01.
I listen carefully ... it was custom made for me.
The words say, "stand by me ... stand by me." There is no voice, nothing to see,
there is only one person it can be ... hope builds inside of me.
The song ends and then nothing more ... the days pass one by one.
The phone rings once again, the time is 12:01. I wonder ... could it be him?
"Hello," I say and once more the music starts to play.
I know he is reaching out to me ... for the song says,
"stand by me," quietly I answer, "I will, I have, I do."
I say, "talk to me." And another song is played.
The words say, "I love you."
My heart knows this is true and hope is renewed.
Into the darkness of the night I whisper, "honey I love you too."
Call number three came more swiftly, it must mean that he needed me.
The music starts to play and I wait patiently,
"wait ... please don't go ... talk to me."
He finally replied and all hope died. A nightmare was building inside.
The voice was wrong ... the only right thing had been the songs.
Contradictions everyone ... the calls had not come from you.
A total stranger now knew ... how very much I loved you.
A faceless stranger without a name,
had heard my voice ... filled with pain,
as I asked you to love me ... once again.
I'm filled with sadness ... I'm filled with sorrow,
and now I am filled with shame.
The stranger with his games ... violated me and used your name.
I woke to sunshine and to pain ... the contradictions came once again.
I was remembering.
The love songs came from a faceless stranger ... without a name,
using my heart ... to play his games.
The midnight caller is not to blame ... I waited for you and I waited in vain.
I waited for a sign ... that never came.
Midnight caller ... please go away. I can handle no more pain.

Answers

I woke up this morning with a smile upon my lips,
and then I reached out and reality hit.
Your pillow was wet, with the tears that I shed,
for I had been dreaming you were safe in our bed.
My arms are empty ... my heart in retreat,
for you always made promises ... that you failed to keep.
So my sweet darling ... please let love go,
for I cannot carry this sorrow ... anymore.
Last night alone, I wandered ... from room to empty room.
The boxes are all packed ... and I'll be leaving soon.
Behind I'll leave the memories ... of a love that never was,
for you failed to believe ... in the strength of our love.

Tears

I could not let you see the tears I cried.
I was too old to cry,
and the tears I'd shed before,
were not the tears of pride.
They have yet to heal the pain I hide.
Tears ... useless tears,
every drop a part of me ... torn apart.
They never solve a thing,
they are but a reminder of the pain,
that memory brings.
No ... I could not let you see,
that there were tears ... left in me.
I could not share my vulnerability.
To face tomorrow and survive,
the reality of tears ... is a truth I must deny.

If All The World Were Green

Imagine: Falling asleep in the darkness that we know as night and awakening to a world with only green. Outside your door, your garden with all its different shapes and sizes lies covered in a sheen of green. There is no definition, no pops of colour, one plant just blending into another. There is no wonder on the individuality of each tender flower. No joy, no inspiration, no beauty. That loss would be ours.

Imagine: The pines and oaks, the maples and elms, the white barked birch have quietly disappeared into the colour green. We see not their beauty, but only a distant memory of that which has been. This leaves us with really nothing ... actually to see. A darkness has crossed before our eyes ... the colour green.

There would be: No shades of light after the darkness of night. The sky has disappeared as if it had never been, lying now in a sea of green. Dawns awakening is gone with no promise of it ever having been. The sun does not rise, it lies lost and forgotten in clouds of green.

There is little hope of sunsets streaking dramatically across our sky in colours of red, orange and shades of pink. Their beauty, their magic, lost and forgotten. There would be no sand dunes running down to waters blue. No crested waves riding the suns light. **We can no longer see ... that which is lost.** The miracles have ended the **wonder** that has filled our life with adventure, and questions and the desire to reach for new horizons ... has gone, lost in a fog of green. We cannot see birds in flight, we hear only the mixture of each birds distinct call. Their physical beauty has disappeared. We have only their music that fills our ears.

Something vital is missing.

Imagine: There are no stars that fill our nights for stars reflect light. These too are gone; mixed only in smokey green. Unseen, beyond our reach. We are left with nothing to reach for, to dream about, to want. There is nothing left to want ... for all we have got ... is something the same. Green. There is no need to travel to far away countries, for we will discover nothing new, only the green left behind ... upon our new world. We stay rooted in one spot, no desire, no imagination, no dreams. We wonder about ... lost in murky green, searching for the elusive: **"more."**

If the flowers in our garden cannot be seen, then the people of the world must all be the same, with no colour, no individuality, no ethnic truth for the destinct possibilities ... that once had been. These individual meaning all of us, with quests, inventions and exceptional talents ... who create the miracles that we have come to expect, have all disappeared, lost in the sameness of earth's green. Not seen, (unseen).

And so the world at large has failed to explore: the God given gift of a life made whole. There is nothing left for us to reach for, to search for, to explore. Can we not learn to share ... the amazing gift of: more.

To be embracing our differences, opening our hearts, and always searching for truth ... leads to a life "well lived."

Can we seriously ... ask for more ... than this?

Otherwise, we ourselves, may ... cease to **exist**, if all the world were green.

Life's Awkward Journey

Looking back down through the years it seems that I started as a tiny bud, tightly closed and surrounded by protective petals like walls to keep me safe. I had been asleep. One morning in the warmth of the suns rays ... my petals opened one by one. I awakened to my first day of being totally alone ... **in the real world** ... to make my own way.

The strength and beauty that was deep within, emerged, energized and exploded as this great adventure into the unknown began. This was all new to me. It did not seem to matter how humble were my beginnings ... what knowledge I would gain ... how strong or frail I was. Once awakened and forced to leave my sheltered life, the pathways that I found to follow ... led me on a "**journey of discovery**" that has blown the cobwebs from my mind.

In time I discovered that I exist for this. I had no compass to guide me on this unknown journey. I had no expectations of what wonders I might find or how scary it could be. Like thistle down ... the breezes carried me to new discoveries and a world that could be construed ... as upside down. I found that it all depended on my point of view and that point of view ... was all up to me. Freedom of choice. Free agency. What will my real life choices be?

With each uncertain step I took I was challenged and rose to the challenge. What else could I do? Choices were all around me and all those choices were mine. What would the results be ... good ... bad ... happy ... sad? I would soon see that life was a mixed bag of reality. It was a learning curve infringing on the paths I wished to travel. It was demanding and it was beautiful.

My life was unexpected ... challenging ... and full of wonder. There was a whole world out there that I knew nothing about. As my paths wandered to places unknown with hills to climb and meadows gentle, I found at last "**my own rhythm.**" I made my own decisions and I learned from my own mistakes.

I uncovered someone that I might never have known and I rejoiced in the person that I found. I had survived. I could stand proud. Life is an "**awkward journey**" not to be missed.

FEATHERED & FURRY FRIENDS

In Memory Of...

Cleopatra
(On Cat Sitting)

It's morning come a calling time and I am refusing to open my eyes, putting off the inevitable. I can feel morning. It comes quietly through my windows. Shreds of daylight slip through chinks in blinds, stealing into darkened corners and shifting night to lighter shades and shadows. As the night evaporates, morning rubs against my eyelids and tugs impatiently at my lashes. I snuggle deeper under the covers, refusing to be disturbed and yet I am.

The window is open just a fraction and a cool breeze slips across my skin, caressing, leaving delicious spots of cold on fingers and nose. I stretch, pushing gently against the cat at my feet. She uncurls, emitting a soft little "purr" at the intrusion. Her paws knead the covers protecting my toes. She digs deep. Quickly I take a peek. Her body is tense as she leaps from bed to dresser to window sill. With tiny nose pressed tight against the window pane, her long tail twitches restlessly, her ears like tiny antenna ... peak. Softly she speaks. "Meow."

I feign sleep. I wait and am not disappointed. One huge paw ... pats against the unopened window, again and again. I smile and hide my head under the sheet. She leaves the window in a single bound with one giant leap and pounces like a heavy boulder upon my bed. The mattress sinks beneath her weight. My smile deepens and my hand affectionately rubs her stubborn little head. She refuses to "purr." Her long tail snaps with impatience. Flipping the covers back, I slip out of bed searching for slippers to ward off the cold.

She flies from the bed and along the hall. She's at the back door in no time at all and there she sits with eyes alert. She knows that I am coming and she crowds the door. Playfully I shove her out of the way. "You be a good girl." The door opens just a crack and she is out, walking majestically, from shadow into the suns light.

She is a work of art, stretching long and sleek , a big ... strong ... powerful ... spoiled ... feline ... with "ATTITUDE."

The Hunter

The little black truck slowed to a stop at the side of the road.
Swinging the door open a young man and his dog jumped clear.
Reaching inside he lifted his rifle and slung it over his shoulder.
With his hand holding firm to the leash man and dog,
strode to the edge of the wood and disappeared.
The man stepped lightly on leaf strewn ground,
downwind ... making no sound.
Clothing blending ... body bending ... beneath the boughs.
The hound ... nose to the ground ... zig zagged at his side,
excitement in the strained lines of her body.
The trail they followed was fresh ... the rabbit scent strong.
With a consistent tug on the lead ... the hound was in pursuit.
The leash unsnapped ... she moved away ... eager for the chase.
The young man waited ... watching ... listening,
as the sound of the howling hound ... grew fainter.
He smiled knowing this could be her last run,
and she was the hunter ... doing what she loved.

A Letter to Our Girl: The Seasons of Your Life

"Paige"

You came to us in the spring. So cute and cuddly and full of life. At first you would hide under the table and sit at the other end of the couch. You were unsure about your new home.

In a short span of time it all changed and you wanted to be with us constantly. We did not go anywhere without thinking of your needs. We made sure that you were safe. When we would return home you were so excited to see us. You would speak to us with your whine and wiggle your body around and around. In later years your response intensified with a voice that we could understand, the squinting of your eyes and the tap, tap, tap of your tail. Our hearts had become intertwined and we felt about you the same way you felt about us. You would comfort us when we were sad and place your head on our knee to let us know that your cared.

You came to us in the spring and our love for you grew. We are so thankful for the memories that we created together. The many walks we took and the playtimes in the park. You so looked forward to catching your frisbee and playing with Sampson. You loved the Christmas season when you were so eager to find and rip open your Christmas presents and sometimes the presents of others. In the evening you would find us so that we could go downstairs to play. You would tug at your toys and chase us from one end of the room to the other. That is about the only time you would bark. You especially loved to steal our gloves and socks and try to run away with them.

Although you had a circle of dog friends, you were a people dog. You would sooner be with people than dogs. Everyone in the neighbourhoods that we lived in over the years knew who you were. We made so many friends because of you. You greeted others with kindness and love. Your mom always said that you were more human than animal. Over your lifetime you have crossed the boundaries of the animal world into the human world and have become part of our eternal family.

You came to us in the spring and we have enjoyed the seasons of your life. On the day we took you to the doctor we expected the worse. We did not know just how ill you were because you never gave a whimper when we went for a walk of played with your toys. When the doctor told us that you were struggling so much, we felt selfish for keeping you for so long and perhaps prolonging your suffering. Please forgive us if that was the case. We did not want to let you go. We knew that you were aware of what was happening on the day that you left us. As you sat between us, with our hands touching you, your life slipped away and your spirit was no longer with us. You accepted it so graciously and I know it was because you did not want us to feel sad. However, it was sadness that we felt as we entered our empty home and you were no longer there. There was no tap, tap, tap of your paws on the floor. There was no wagging tail. Some of the love had left our home.

Paige you came to us in the spring and even though you were only with us for twelve short years, it seems like there was never a time when you weren't with us. Now that you are gone, there is a place in our hearts that could only be filled by you. It has only been a short time since we have been apart since you have left us but there isn't a day that goes by that we don't think of you. We hope that you are running like the wind and catching frisbees in Heaven.

Oh, we would love to catch one more glimpse of your precious face but we know it would have been unfair of us to expect you to continue to suffer with the ailments of your mortal body. We are just so thankful that you were able to move with us to our new home. Sometimes, we think that you stayed with us just long enough to know where we were so you could visit us when you wanted. Even though we won't be able to see you, we will feel your presence because you are unforgettable.

Paige you came to us in the spring and you left us in the spring but oh what joy and love we shared through the seasons of your life. We will love you forever. As we stroll along the path in the evening, we see puppies everywhere, puppies that give great pleasure to those who love them the most.

Love ... your eternal family

- Written by Max Barter to his Wife Pamela ... "A Christmas Memory with Love."

The Seagull

To fly ... to dip ... to soar.
To be carried weightless upon the wind.
To climb high and disappear into the endless sky.
To pass squaking and bank towards the shore.
To lightly touch down.
To stand proudly upon the sands,
to step into the waves.
To strut ... to search ... to demand.
To lift ... to glide ... to skim ... waters blue.
To conquer earth ... sea ... sky.
To have the freedom to fly.

To Catch a Sunbeam

From seemingly out of nowhere, as if blown by the wind, a small ball of fluff came rolling across the shining kitchen floor. Helter-skelter, slip-sliding and colliding with the kitchen chair.

The sunbeams reflections left darting patterns in the air and shadows played every where. The coloured ball uncurled from its position on the floor and hurled its tiny weight high into the air. He missed the sunbeam which disappeared only to appear again somewhere. With head tilted at a crazy angle ... confused blue eyes followed the dancing beam until it stopped to rest suddenly a few floor tiles away.

Padded feet moved silently as he stalked his prey and with a final lunge ... head down in ramming position ... furry paws released tiny claws to catch the elusive light.

It was as if the light had never been, for the sky had carried it around the corner of the house.

We only saw the back end of our little soft bomb as he exploded ... paws flailing under the counter. He was done in. He lay in a relaxed heap ... unmoving. His mother washed her kitten where he slept. He'd had a busy day ... chasing sunbeams ... that never stayed.

With loving hands the artist followed the flowing curves of cat and kitten. The picture in his mind was beautiful and he recreated that picture forever in the warm dark wood ... and then he put his tools away.

The message is clear. Whatever the heart and mind can conceive and believe, it can achieve. There is order ... harmony ... love, in the universe ... do not despair.

Mother Love

The branches snapped like twigs before the power of the grisley who lumbered into the clearing. Pursuing her victim she easily shortened the distance.

Her tremendous weight ... landed full upon her captive and her huge paws, raised him high into the air ... then dropped him in a strangle hold upon her massive chest.

They rolled and spun about ... inseparable ... and he clung with limbs flung about her neck. The mighty roar of the grisley, reached the stillness of the wood and the forest creatures awaiting the outcome.

Exhausted she rolled unto her back ... a look of contentment upon her face ... and the bundle she held in her arms was a miniature like unto herself. The cub snuggled deeper into her neck ... conent to sleep after their play.

The artist captured the moment perfectly and carved it lovingly into the once lifeless wood ... and the carving stood, "TO MOTHER LOVE."

Pixie

A little ball of fluff and feathers
yellow, white and grey.

With inquisitive questioning eyes, a tilted head,
a talent for mimicking and wings to fly.

A songbird, a pet,
unpredictably totally loveable.

She makes us laugh with her musical talent.
A pecking order upon a mirror ... in time ... to a song.

A small perfect package of joy and wonder.

A gift of happiness freely given.
A tiny miracle, precious,
part of a family.

LIFE LESSONS

Acts of Love

Touch not with darkness ... the beauty of another's soul,
but gently bring it to you and wrap it around your own.
Touch not with anger ... a heart that is cracked and broke,
but gather it closer ... with kind and loving strokes.
Touch not with disbelief ... a faith that stands firm,
but reach towards that light ... grasp it ... learn.
Touch not with accusation ... a spirit that is low,
but offer protection, kindness, laughter, hope and joy.
Always treat another's heart ... as if it were your own,
and surprisingly ... joy will be your reward.
Offer to another ... the selfless love you seek,
and heal your own heart ... with the blessings you will reap.
Look for strength and goodness ... and peace and love will follow,
and your confusion will be ... no more.
The storms that have been raging ... these will pass,
and within a heart that knows your own,
you will find a love that lasts.
Beyond all your trials ... one constant truth remains,
you are worthy of a love ... that only you can name.

Fair Weather Friend

I ask you ... where were you,
in the darkness that was my night?
When I screamed for help and no one heard my plight?
When I was too weak ... even to fight?
Where were you then ... on those lonely, lonely nights?
I ask you ... where were you when daylight broke,
and all the world awoke with hope?
I watched the sun rise ... and could not rise with the sun,
for my eyes were closed ... with salted tears,
and my heart was heavy ... with my fears.
Where were you then ... all those lonely, lonely years?
I ask you once again ... where were you my friend,
when my life changed ... and I did not?
When my world was gone ... while I lived in it?
When my body was wracked with pain,
and I thought ... I would go insane?
Where were you then ... my fair weather friend?
What gives you the right ... to judge the hell I've been through,
for I never once ... got any help from you.
Where were you when I needed you ... where were you then?

Sleeping Beauty
(My Window View)

Life lessons can be hard sometimes but personally I stubbornly effused to ignore what I had see and lived through and felt, for I knew it was all part of the "**human experience**" and now a vital part of my own Reality.

For your information "**Sleeping Beauty**" had awakened and was gratefully letting go of her "**fairytale**" existence. Her life had been too happy, too simple, too protected for far too long. Now ... having tasted life as it was meant to be lived, with all its many challenges, dangers, possibilities and decisions, with mistakes waiting to happen and successes to be achieved, there was no way that, "**Sleeping Beauty**," was retreating back to "**safe**." That destructive action would never again come into play.

So here I was in the real world where there was no place left to hid and I had no desire to do so.

I finally understood that I was meant to make this journey from start to finish and I did not want it any other way. Where there was pain there would be the wonder of survival, mixed with unbelievable strength. Confusion would give way to clear vision as my mind began to play with a multitude of possible solutions. Choices were scattered all around me leaving me with no reason to fear ... anything at all. Time would always be slipping away and so procrastination was not a viable commodity.

I knew I needed to be happy and I would continue to pursue this elusive something. I began to see that happy ... needed to start with me. So simple really. I had been happy many times before, why not once more? It was definitely worth searching for.

One thing I understood for certain was that ... "**I must not judge**." I could try to help others but I was unworthy to judge them. It was wrong that I should even attempt judgement when I had not walked the paths they trod, knew not the trials and struggles they faced or the enemies real or imagined ... that they fought. Naturally "**love**" should be our weapon of choice. It is the strongest force I know ... with the least harm done. I must remember this.

"I Hear You"

"I hear you," she said to the sweetheart of her youth, but she didn't speak the truth. She was busy baking bread and had not heart a word he'd said. "Of course I'm listening," she answered once again as she ran for the phone. "I'm here, I'm home," but all he ever felt in this house ... was alone.

"I'm coming," she said as he waited patiently, but she forgot about him and was lost to the story that she read.

One day he came home, head hanging low, shoulders slumped and feet dragging slow. They met at the door, "something awful happened at work today. I need to talk to you right away." She stopped in her tracks, looked at him and said, "I understand, I'll just be a minute and I'll be right back."

He watched as she walked away. She never listened to a word he'd say. It seemed it had always been this way. He watched till she was out of sight. The minutes stretched, somehow into hours. He was deep in thought. He took a second to look at the clock. His Life was ticking away. He could no longer live this way.

He packed his clothes that night and stepped into the darkness of the night. It felt good and it was right.

She came home to find that she was all alone and on the table by the phone the note said, "I hear you too and I also understand, but I am no longer waiting. I've done all I can."

As the words reached her heart, her thought echoed in the dark ... "I'm listening Sweetheart." but there was no one to hear and the cold she felt ... was mixed with fear.

(A thoughtless way to lose love in a relationship.)

An Opportunity for Change

A blank piece of paper with no words left to write.
A life in turmoil ... no answer right.
A heart in pieces ... beyond repair,
faith wavering ... no answer there.
Courage turned to despair ... a lost soul wanders there.
Truth becomes a matter of conjecture ... changed by a point of view,
but whose?
We try ... we win ... we fail ... we lose,
choices matter .... I'm confused.
Memories of yesterdays ... its warmth ... its light,
contradict today's plight.
If nobody is wrong ... name the enemy we fight.
Too many variables make up the pattern of our lives.
We fought the battles ... carried the pain,
and now wear the scars.
Too many mistakes made ... to change the outcome after all.
We win ... we lose ... we try ... we fail,
is there anyone left who really cares?
I hear the world awakening ... beyond my window-pane.
A new day dawns ... the nightmare fades.
Today ... is an opportunity for change.

Letting Go

You still come unannounced ... as my first waking thought,
and you are forever in my prayers.
I ask not for me now ... only that you will be happy,
someday ... somehow.
The nightmare continues ... but its not so scary now,
for I understand where you have gone ... the why ... the how.
I am letting go,
for I will not follow ... the paths of your tortured mind,
And I realize your nightmares ... were never mine.
I am letting go,
so you can wander ... in your nowhere land,
your haven from all harm.
The whys to all my questions ... are so simply explained.
Your poor battered heart ... can handle no more pain.
You cannot comprehend ... from out of your twisted past,
that what I offered you ... was a love that would last.
I am letting go ... because I love you ... and you said NO!

Highway to Nowhere

Two hearts collide ... from distant skies,
travelling on a highway to nowhere
just for a moment ... time coincides ... stops and solidifies,
and holds them together.
In the same frame of mind ... hands touch and entwine,
eyes lock and visions clear ... they talk, they hear and they understand.
The merging is natural ... simple ... beautiful,
like sunlight filtering through rose petals.
Harmony and joy surround them ... while all around them,
people and time ... are passing.
Yet this moment cannot last ... the past is not the past.
There ahead ... the road divides.
In a moment ... the moment will be over.
Again they will travel ... alone ... on a highway to nowhere.
One heart hurts ... the other does not comprehend,
what has transpired.
He continues to walk AHEAD ... towards his past,
leaving the LIGHT ... behind him.
He walks alone ... with only his SHADOW to guide him,
travelling on a highway ... to nowhere.

Love Died

Love died ... I think it died,
this beautiful feeling ... deep inside,
dried up and died.
I didn't even see it go ... until one morning I awoke,
and knew that it was so.
Love died ever so slowly ... with every tear I cried,
through all the pain ... I tried to hide.
Was it your thoughtlessness ... to everything I represent,
the underlying coldness ... that was present,
the taking of all I had to give ... that did not allow ... love to live?
Love died ... how could it survive,
when every act of love ... I gave to you ... was tossed aside,
and every truth I spoke ... you twisted and denied,
until the tenderness from within ... was cut in tiny ribbons?
Love died ... and I didn't even see it go,
until one morning I awoke ... and knew that it was so.
There are no tears left to cry ... no need left ... to say goodbye.
No reason to hold this pain within.
Love died ... because it was denied ... and that's the greatest sin,
for LOVE ... is everything.

Self Exploration

Life is like a jigsaw puzzle to be explored, dissected, unravelled and put back together but perhaps not always in the same old way. Life is complicated. I recently decided to ask the simple question, "**why**." It was opening up windows and doors to my mind. Expanding on unanswered questions.

I realized at any early age that I lived by my own set of rules, concepts, thoughts. In many ways I was untried, young , naïve. In many other ways I was ahead of my years. I was comfortable in my own skin. My thoughts had a way of rearranging the events of my day to fit into a pattern that I could accept. I had no problems being on my own. I love to lay on the grass down by the creek and listen to the thoughts that circle in my head while birds circled overhead. I seemed to have no problems interacting with friends. Perhaps I was an old soul. Now I am just rather old.

Understanding me certainly is not a necessity for you. How absurd that would be.

Understanding you however is a whole different story. Ask if you have looked inside your heart, soul and mind lately. It's always good to remember to check occasionally. Perhaps you should search out your own defining moments, your inspiration and your strengths. That is what matters here. How do you think? Why do you do what you do? What triggers your reactions to certain buttons that "**rock your world?**" Is it possible for you to turn it around and come at it from a different angle? Do not be a puppet on a string for you are in control of your own words, actions, destiny. These are precious **gifts from God to you**. Remember that you matter.

Remember always if you can ... "**to be kind**," If someone is making you unhappy, imagine just how unhappy that person must be. **How sad from them**! If it is possible, turn it around and pay it forward. Make a difference if you can and yet realize, "**you are not responsible for their happiness**."

We are linked together in some form or other at some time in the here and now or a future we cannot name. It's known as "**the human condition**." We are all a part of this. We cannot divest ourselves of **the responsibility** that each of us carries, for what we do and say regardless of our **intentions**, will always have a rippling effect on others. Like the canoe in still waters, with the movement of the paddle we create a ripple and with the next pull ... we have a wave.

Undoubtedly this will impact each of our lives in countless unknown ways. Actions of any kind equal reactions and as we all react differently to any given action ... like a tidal wave this can swamp us. We must individually hold onto the **memory of self** for future reference, lest we forget ... just who we are.

Who we are matters greatly. Happiness matters greatly. Without this we could not survive. To not search for both would be a colossal waste of a life. Do not let it be your life. Something to think about.

There I go again lost on the merry-go-round called internalization. Flights of fancy travelling through time to this particular page. It seems my mind and fingers search out my thoughts regardless of my best intentions.

Only With Words

" I love you," he said to the woman in his arms.
"I love you true ... how could you doubt the words I speak to you?"
Sadly she shook her head and turned her eyes away,
for he only loved her ... on his appointed days.
She had given up her dreams ... of forever and always.
It was not going to happen ... not now ... not ever.
She did not fully understand,
why love for her was somehow ... banned.
For her it seemed ... it was love on demand.
"I love you" he said as he kissed her long and sweet.
But her heart was not in it ... her heart was in retreat.
"Do you love me too?" he whispered in her ear.
She answered softly, "yes my dear ... loving you was my greatest fear."
Her heart lay frozen in her breast ... attesting to her loneliness.
That tears that did not fall ... scarred a heart ... past all recall.
"I love you" he said, "but its getting late,
and I have things to do that cannot wait."
She locked the door on his goodbye ... and then she locked her heart away.
"I love you too,"
she whispered into the darkness of the night,
"I really do ... that is my truth."

CIRCLE OF ABUSE

Circle of Abuse

Abuse comes in many forms. Quite often the abuser is unaware that their actions are abusive. Abuse could be part of a learned behaviour quite often during childhood. Many times it occurs because they have been hurt or were traumatized by some event beyond their control.

Silence: is one form of abuse. **Criticism and constant put downs:** another. **Isolation:** is really rather scary for there is nobody to turn to for help and quite often ... this is the plan.

(**"I'm shouting here, victims beware."**)

Mind games: can play havoc with your sanity. There are so many forms of **Fear:** to be inflicted upon those that are defenseless and without hope. Know that **accidents can happen:** yet most times recurring accidents are "**not self inflicted.**"

Bruises: can be hidden and **Broken limbs:** explained but **the scars within ... keep right on "hurting." Stalking:** is a whole other kettle of fish. There is no excuse for **Temper or anger:** that results in **physical violence.**

Sexual abuse: is not the **right** of one Human Being over Another.

Family and friends may be totally unaware of the "**plight of the victim**," whom they love ... for the **abuser** shows to the world a completely different and usually beautiful individual. In this regard ... those that could possibly help often turn away ... for they do not **believe** ... that the abuse is real.

Unless abused ourselves none of us can really understand the massive damage that occurs to the victim. To ask for help is most often not something the "**victims of abuse**" can do. This statement is true. They are afraid of repercussions and sometimes also ashamed ... for over time they have come to believe that somehow; they ... themselves ... are to blame.

This thought process is so very wrong!

The **victim** should never be **blamed**. How do we stop the **insanity**? On the outside looking in ... how do we approach it? Where do we even begin? I do know that the threats are real and the scars that are left ... **sometimes never heal**.

Agencies for the Abused:
Hospitals ... Doctors ... Nurses
Social Services ... Women's Shelters
Local Police Services ... Churches

(Do not suffer in silence, help is near.)

Driftwood

From where did you come on your journey to me?
How far have you travelled ... what have you seen?
From what distant shore ... did you embark?
From what branch of which tree ... were you torn apart?
All I see now ... is your beauty.
Tell me, were you storm tossed ... rough handled ... wave licked?
Did you bump along the bottom ... or was your journey quick?
Were you always ... alone ... lost ... or in pain?
What are you feeling ... what is your name?
All I see now ... is your beauty.
I found you on the shore ... on a perfect summer day,
wrapped in warm grains of sand ... healing in the suns soft rays.
My hands are gentle ... my heart is strong,
I want to take your home ... where you belong.
Life's journey brought you to me ... all I see now ... is your beauty.
God creates miracles ... for those who believe.
You are the miracle ... God gave to me.

(Confronted with the reality of abuse I found.)
(I started paying attention.)

Stalked

She walked always with shadows, searching crowds for a certain face, size, shape. Holding herself ready for confrontations ... at any time and in any place. She never **relaxed** ... she never felt **safe**. She drove fast, checking the road ahead, the streets behind, the side roads converging, expecting to see a little black car with a lone grey -haired driver ... slipping in behind her.

Her home was no longer a haven. The outer doors not always secured. Automatically as she crossed the threshold ... she turned and locked and double locked ... and all the while it played upon her nerves ... that those **locks** had become "**her world**." She was always aware of the possibility of danger and there was no peace to be found. She felt ... alone ... abused ... afraid. Nobody knew when or even if the stalker would change his stalking and make his move ... or just what the move might be ... for he was lost in his own, "**world of fantasy**."

His car patrolled her work, her home, her family and friends. The phone invaded her privacy. The **buzzer** shattered the "**darkness of the night**" bringing her awake to helplessness and despair. He was always there ... he was everywhere. He knew when her blinds were open ... when shut, who came to visit an when they went out, which lights were on in which room at what time. He knew more about her life ... than I knew about mine.

What did he want ... when would he stop ... what would he do? The scary part was that nobody knew ... least of all him, for he was "**confused**." From Heaven to Hell ... from freedom to trapped ... she couldn't go forward ... she would never go back. Finally she acknowledged, "**she needed help**." In **humility** she asked ... "to have her **life back**!"

On the outside looking in it is hard to tell where the love stopped and the nightmare began. We have no right to judge or criticize or condemn, for we have not walked ... where the stalked have been. So if you are out there ... alone with your thoughts ... afraid of the sunshine ... afraid in the dark ... find the courage to

"RIGHT THIS WRONG , BE STRONG!"

Reach out your hand and pick up the phone. Someone will answer... someone will hear. We understand that the dangers are real. We know the pain ... confusion ... fear. You are not alone ... help is near.

Stand and fight for your "**RIGHT TO CHOOSE A LIFE OF YOUR OWN**."

The Artful Deceiver

She wears two faces but only one does she allow the world to see, for she keeps her **secrets safe, close** and her **goals are:**

"ULTIMATE POWER AND CONTROL"

She plays the **Saint** beautifully, forever **helpful**, Without **complaint, human**. The **victim** she plays with nuance **ripe, tragic**.

She can **manufacture** hurt, pain, loss and tears **upon command**, winning **hearts** she can **manipulate and turn around**.

Quite often what we see and witness are **not real emotions** but an **anger she cannot control**, against those who see her **clearly, and refuse to play her games**.

The followers ... the sheep, that trot along behind with their **hearts open** and **bleeding** for the supposed injustice and cruelty their **leader portrays**, rise **blindly to her defence**. Their **rational minds** are **lost**. They get **tangled** in a web so fine, "like the **spider to the fly**" and they are truly lost. Gone perhaps forever. **How sad**.

They become a **group of militants**, with a just cause and a need to **fight** and **destroy**. They are filled with **hate** and supposed "**justified justice**." They become someone they never wanted or even thought they could be, "**just puppets on a string**," who dance upon command ... deftly **played** by a

master mind ... with no shame.

Does anyone ever win? Do you remember the goal: **ultimate power and control!** The little general ... pulling the:

"**strings** of "**LOST SOULS.**"

Heart of a Child

The heart of a child ... torn in two, by both opposing ... points of view.
Now ... hurting, afraid, confused, while the battle rages overhead,
she hears every word in anger said.
Loving you both ... what can she do ... why must you make her choose.

Are you listening ... do you hear?
Do you see her ... standing near?

How is it possible she will survive, without scars ... carved deep inside?
This priceless bundle ... now aged five, the gift you were given ... multiplied.
With big trusting eyes ... a sunny smile, her joyous laughter ... her quiet prayer,
the tiny child ... whose heart must heal,
needs to walk into tomorrow ... without fear.

Are you listening ... do you hear?
Do you see her ... standing near?

Just Pondering

Unexpectedly the unthinkable happens and the earth falls away beneath your feet and you go down hard. You are **confused, hurt** and yes **angry** while trying to understand and piece together the role that was played that changed the safety of your world. **"Forever friends"** there is no security in this statement.

They banded together, put you on **trial** and **convicted** you. The outcome was: **PRE-DETERMINED … THE TRIAL RIGGED … THE CONVICTION BOGUS.** Who does that? They were of one mind or perhaps, led by just one mind. Half a century of ups and downs, challenges and victories held together by a handful of hearts. Where are those hearts now?

You seek for answers within and come up empty. Forgiveness for them is necessary for my survival. I know this but have not yet arrived at this point. I have many questions that need to be answered ... or perhaps forgotten. I will get there.

Emotions raged amid disinformation subtle enough to move mountains and the perception of once intelligent people. I was clueless as to why and what. I do know that the personalities of those who have gone, have changed but not for the better. I wonder who changed them? I wonder if this makes them happy? Is this what they wanted? **Just pondering!**

Looking down through the years I remember others that have been swept aside, lost, tumbled and I realize that I am not alone in this **particular storm**.

From a storm in a tea-cup to a raging hurricane you disappear into oblivion. Has justice been served? Was it even considered? Not really. You analyze how strong intelligent friends have been swept up and have **allowed such manipulation**, the **finality** of which is devastating to you ... **the target**.

What will the future hold for them. I wonder. **Whose loss is it really?** In the midst of the storm you realize that you are no longer confused. You may hurt but you won't break. It's not allowed. When rational thought disappears and nothing makes sense you hold firm to the truth within and move forward to a better tomorrow. You are no longer lost and just a little sad but determined to **"sorrow no more."** Life is everchanging, a learning tool, a chance to grow. **Perhaps lost friends was a GIFT.** Who knew!

I step with strength into the great unknown ... with all the choices in the world at my feet. I am free and happy.

"Clear Vision"

I was but a little man ... spouting words of scripture,
I did not ... fully understand.
Wielding power ... with a heavy hand,
pulling strings ... so they jumped to my commands.
In the end. Alone I stand,
the gifts of family ... God given ... gone!
Control is wrong ... isolation cruel.
Humble now I know ... only LOVE should rule.
Give this man ... just one more chance.
I need ... I want ... my family back.
In the mirror I clearly see ... who I no longer want to be.
Forgive me please ... for now I know,
true strength lies ... not in control!
I can promise only ... to love you more.
I was but a little man ... now I fully understand,
I want to be quite simply ... all you need.
Again I ask ... **FORGIVE ME PLEASE**.

The Eye of the Storm

A child races blindly in the forest below ... **lost ... alone ... confused ... afraid**. The storm rages and swirls about him. A cold rain soaks the earth ... turning the path to mud.

Tiny feet slow ... bogged down in slippery soil. He falls and does not rise. Cold, soaked to the skin ... exhausted and without hope ... healing sleep envelopes him. The wind howls ... branches bend ... leaves fall upon the tiny body below. The coloured tapestry keeps him warm. The **"love of God"** surrounds him.

The "**storm**" moves on ... **unaware of the harm done!**

Peace ... returns to the forest. Starlight keeps watch ... on the boy through the night. As always after the darkness ... **there is light, a miracle ... a gift given ... a new day**. Birds sing in branches high ... drops of rain ... slide down tree trunks wide. A squirrel chatters by his side.

The "**child**" awakes, sits up rubbing his eyes. The leaves scatter. **Hope through innocence** survives. He stands, stretches, reaching high, then follows the sunlight dancing by. He reaches the edge of the forest ... the meadow lays before him. He skips ... he runs ... he slides.

A **child** caught in the ... **eye of the storm** any storm from **forces within or without**, deserves the "**miracle of love**" to come through it, intact ... healthy ... happy ... safe ... alive. A child is a **miracle** full of wonder and light, given to us to nurture and protect, keep safe not neglect. We as **parents** are the "**keepers of the light**." To keep them safe is their ... "**God given right**."

The Rivers Edge

She stands alone on the banks of the river,
her face lifted toward the last rays of the sun.
Its warmth ... its beauty ... fails to heal,
all the hurting, hidden, places within.
She is lost in a nightmare that never ends.
She shivers and pulls her sweater closer about her,
to hold off the cold ... but the cold lies within.
Isolated in a place far from family and friends,
with a phone that never rings,
she remembers many things.
The hopes and dreams ... not fulfilled,
that she shared with a husband ... long gone,
selfishly following ... dreams of his own.
She allows her mind to focus on the abuse down through the years.
The hidden tears ... the grief she could not ... would not share.
What she might have done to stop the tragedy,
to stand up and face reality ... to free self and family,
from a marriage gone wrong ... this she could not do.
That is the sad ... unspoken ...hidden ... truth.
Sunshine sparkling on still waters ... ducks paddling under branches low,
peace and beauty at the rivers edge ... as day fades slowly into the night.
She stands ... alone and cold ... and without hope.
When will she see,
that the answers are within ... as they have always been.

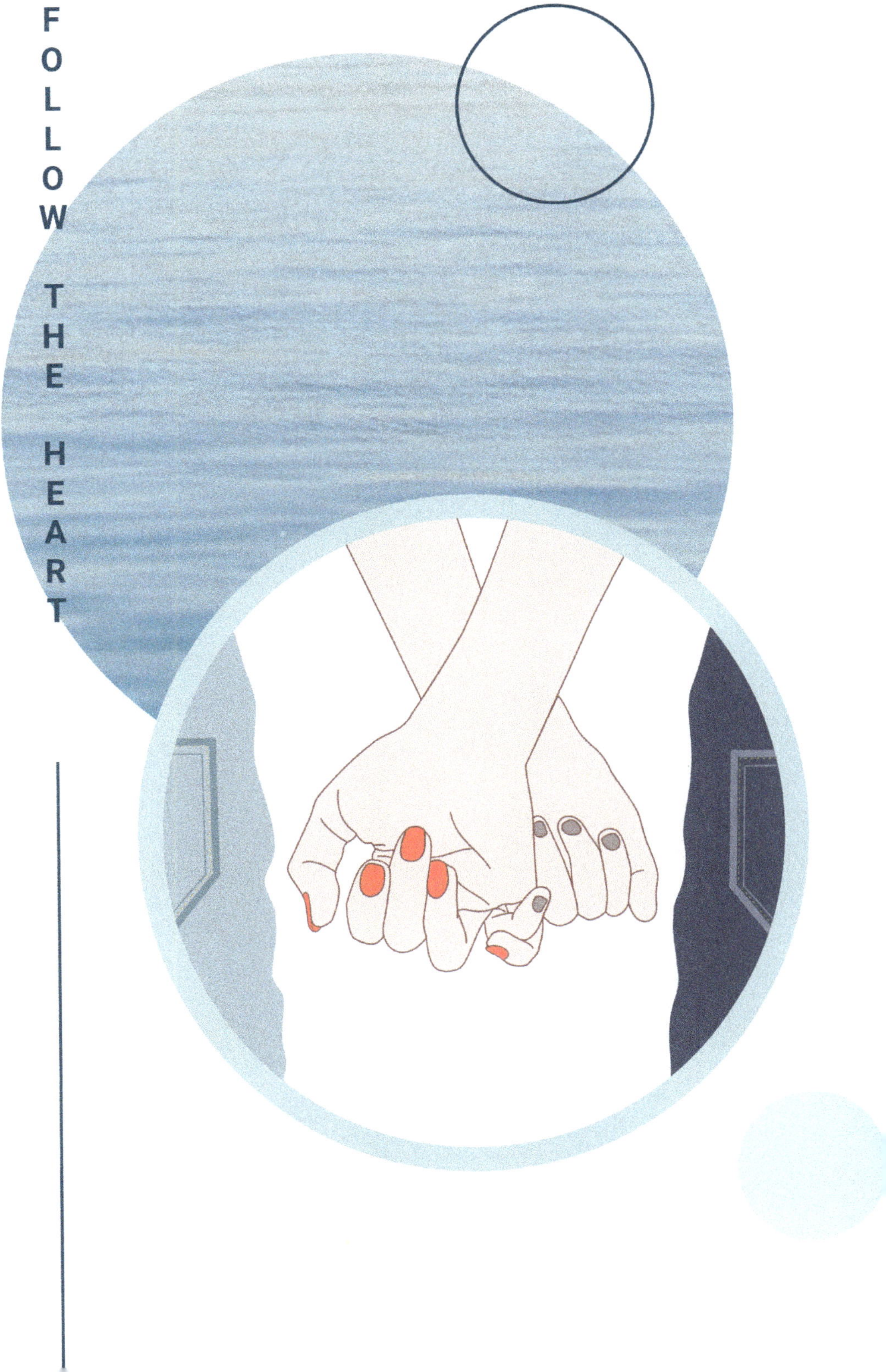
FOLLOW THE HEART

Touch Me

Travel gently across the trails of my heart,
enter softly Sweetheart.
Trace the line upon a face no longer young,
if you find beauty ... it must be love.
Touch with wisdom ... my soul,
and explore with me ... the promise of tomorrow.
If on your travels ... you should discover who I am,
fold me with tenderness ... in your arms once again.
I ask here to stay ... to love you always,
in my own special way.

Snap Shot

My eyes like a camera ... focused on the subject.
My body poised ... ready to shoot.
The lens of my mind ... swiftly shut,
and I developed my picture,
in the darkness that was my heart.
It was a picture of him ... now gone,
yet he remains ... imprinted forever,
in the chords ... of my memory.

At Journey's End

I once held life and all its treasures in a heart too big to measure.
Strong though I was one day I awoke ... heart broke.
Lost and all alone ... at journeys end ... I began to build my life again.
My face lay washed in salty tears ... once heart whole ... now I understand fear.
Fine lines of pain appeared and stayed ... eyes that once shone bright,
now held little hope ... and no light.
My heart filled to overflow ... with an emptiness I could not control.
Each day became a reflection ... of another tortured night.
Would tomorrow never come ... to end my plight.
I searched in vain in a world filled with people ... looking for just one thing,
a matching heart with no shame ... and a soul that only love could claim.
The years slipped quickly by ... my faith had all but died.
Still my hungry heart searched on ... for in this crazy world I knew,
somewhere ... waiting ... I would find you.
My journey taught me things I never wanted to know,
it only made me want you more.
Perhaps if I opened just one more door ... give me strength dear Lord.
Then one night I saw you standing there ... perfect ... none compared.
In a room full of people ... heart to heart ... soul to soul,
I needed to know ... nothing more. You entered in through loves open door,
and searched and found my waiting soul. At journey end ... my life began.
I who once held life and all its treasures ... in a heart too big to measure.
Now I hold a treasure true ...life's journey taught me ... the value of you.

My Guy

He touches me in all the hidden places ... the world does not see.
He touches me so tenderly ... with his heart.
He reaches out to me ... so easily,
trusting ... believing that I am ... the woman I profess to be.
He reaches me ... deeply ... with his mind.
He gives to me completely ... and so sweetly,
and as he draws me close ... in his embrace,
I realize it is life itself ... I face.
Do I dare step away from the past,
can I find the strength ... to give you what you ask?
I have been offered ... true love ... at last.

Love is a Miracle

Love is a miracle, a secret smile, a radiance from within.
Love is a song in your heart that does not depart ... life is about to begin.
Words now have meaning ... tenderness is real.
Two hearts are beating ...you actually feel.
Remember hands touching, eyes meeting, hearts reaching.
Harmony ... peace.
As long as you live ... never forget ... for love comes so seldom,
there is no time for regret. Love is a "miracle."

Beyond Words

It's the way you say ... "I love you," with your eyes.
At odd moments I surprise a look ... so full and so deep,
that I feel heaven bound.
It happens always when you are around,
for your love goes beyond words ... I've found.
It's the way you say "I love you" ... with your touch.
For no special reason you reach out,
to let me know you are there ... and that you care.
You fold me in your arms at night,
and all my problems ... drop out of sight,
for your love goes beyond words ... and it feel so right.
It's the way you say "I love you" ... with your smile.
It brings with it all the acceptance ... I will ever need.
It lets me know that you believe ... in who I am.
Your love goes beyond words ... and I pray it never ends.
It's all the little things you do ... that add up to,
the most beautiful ... "I love you."
I thank you with all my heart,
for the priceless "gift of love" ... you brought.

It Was

It was like the sun on a winters day ... warm.
It was like berries ripened in season ... sweet.
It was like the first spring breeze ... fresh.
It was like an infant reaching to be held ... beautiful.
Warm ... sweet ... fresh ... beautiful.
Such was his smile ... I will miss it.

Excellence by Choice

It takes a man of vision ... with wisdom,
to find a woman ... of eternal beauty.
It takes a woman ... of courage and faith,
to wait for ... such a man.

Moment in Time

The sky without a wrinkle of a cloud ... was clear.
The air kissed warm from the sun ... played the breezes that filled the sails.
The little white sloop ... cut through the waters of blue,
and intermixed with it all ... was my awareness of you.
The touch of your hand and mine ... on the tiller.
The warmth of your smile ... the light of quiet acceptance in your eyes.
The sound of your voice mixed with laughter ... our first kiss.
The hope that was born, that lived ... that died,
all in one perfect afternoon.
These are the things ... that I will remember.
These are the things ... that I won't forget.
These are the feelings ... that I have been searching for.
Perhaps someday when I feel worthy ... I will feel these feelings again.
Until then my friend ... thank you for showing me ... them.

Sweetheart

You gave me hope when there was only despair.
You healed a heart ... hurt beyond repair.
I looked past the problems and saw you standing there.
Your love was everywhere ... I knew I cared.
You filled my world ... with happiness,
and I will give to you ... nothing less.
Sweetheart ... I promise you a love that is true.
Trust the feelings ... inside of you.

Only With Love

We've travelled down roads never walked before,
but now we are together and no longer walk alone.
You've shown me a different world ... with new horizons,
and you have become ... my rising sun.
Now when darkness falls ... I fear nothing and no one at all.
You hold me gently in your arms ... and I fall asleep.
It's the memory of your face I keep.
Hold me till morning comes,
I find I need ... your special kind of love.

Remember to Remember

Take the precious time not filled with incidentals,
to recall the beauty of it all ... as we came together.
Remember to stop and look for me ... in the confusion of your day.
Realize that together ... is where we should be.
Search and find the memories ... that are yours and mine.
Take the time to claim the happiness ... these memories unwind.
Remember to remember ... that true love lasts forever.
That the problems of day to day ... fade away ... but the love always stays.
Remember and never forget ... that my heart has no regrets,
and strength enough for two ... if you need it to help you through.
Remember past all your pain ... that love remains,
and beyond your wildest dreams ... the reality of us exists ... it seems.
Remember always to remember ... forgetting never,
for true love ... must be treasured.

Once Upon a Dream

You would have been my mountain high,
and my sheltered Valley,
the pot of gold and the end of the rainbow.
You would have been my deep and still waters,
my green pastures ... my morning sun ... and my moonbeam.
You would have been my best friend ... beautiful lover,
teacher and mate.
I would have been anything and anyone ... you wanted me to be.
Once ... long ago ... upon a dream.

Fatal Attraction

I saw you and you drew me to you.
I met you ...and it increased,
I danced and moved in time with you,
and the beat was true.
I talked and laughed with you ... and knew peace.
It was like coming home ... yet to a home I've never known.
It was like a missing piece ... a puzzle solved,
a flower torn and then reborn.
If only I DARED ... I was SCARED ... I knew I CARED.

Side by Side

As I search to discover your reality,
I can clearly see the beauty ... that you offered me.
I listen to the words you say,
there is no hint of the games ... people play.
I know that you would never ... betray me,
as we walk ... side by side.
My heart reaches out and touches ... your heart,
which reaches out and touches ... every part of me,
and we are two separate entities ... together,
walking side by side and hand in hand.
Joined through acceptance and love,
alike yet different ... different yet the same,
bound together by some force ... we cannot name.
Indivisible by distance or time ... place or people,
as side by side ... hand in hand ... heart to heart,
we walk in love ... towards tomorrow and another tomorrow.

Always with Love

We have climbed mountains high.
Sheltered in Valleys low.
Shared both sorrow and joy.
I will climb any mountain left to climb,
with you by my side,
trusting always ... in the power of two.
I believe in you ... I believe in us,
always ... and with love.

One Day

One day a man will come.
One of strength ... of courage ... of wisdom,
and he will see in me ... all that I am or ever could be.
He will sweep into my life ... and do me the honour,
of being his wife,
and life will be lived ... fulfilled ... as it was meant to be.
And the words that hold meaning are,
trust ... respect ... patience ... love.

The Land of I Love You

Love is a sacred place where two hearts come together,
strengthened by a unique band of understanding.
They stand ... two strong,
against all the things ... that can go wrong.
Love is the place where symphonies ... of harmony are made.
Patience is displayed ... and trust is earned.
Giving ... always is returned.
It's a place where equals ... meet ... speak ... listen,
as they learn ... from one another,
standing strong ... in times of trouble.
Love is a place where laughter ... mingles with tears,
and fears are faced together.
Promises are kept there ... dreams come true.
You will find that empty words ... are not allowed,
in the ... "land of I love you."
It's a sacred place ... and I want to share it,
only and always ... with you.

The Search

I have been searching ... searching for you,
searching for my dream of love ... my whole life through.
I'd meet someone and ask myself ... what about you?
Then I would realize that no ... they would not do,
for I was searching ... searching for you.
The instant that I saw your smile ... I knew,
I needed just to be near to you.
And when you spoke to me ... again I knew,
that this was where I belonged.
I knew ... I knew ... I knew.
For I had been searching for you ... my whole life through.
With all my heart ... I give my love to you,
hoping that you ... have been searching ... for me too.

Friends and Lovers and Friends

He takes me quietly by the hand,
and leads me and gently lays me down.
Then he gathers me to him ... in arms that are strong,
and with hands that are sure ... and I feel wanted and secure.
He nurtures me ... and I come alive ... and I feel the excitement,
for he plays me like ... a finely tuned instrument,
he himself being the great musician,
and the melody is piercing ... yet sweet,
and when the music is over ... it lingers yet awhile,
to filter through our bodies ... and through our minds,
and we are as one ... for this moment in time.
I will remember us always,
as friends and lovers and friends.

Sweet Awakening

We have so little time to reflect, our days and nights are filled,
sometimes to the point of exhaustion ... and yet,
I would not have wanted to miss ... one day of knowing you.
You make the hard days ... bearable ... and the good days ... magical.
You have added ... depth to a world ... superficial,
laughter ... to balance my tears ... steadfastness ... to allay my fears.
My haven from all harm ... is within the circle of your arms.
The strength I first saw in you ... did not peter out and disappear.
I discovered as I drew near ... that your strength ... was real.
You said that loving was found ... in day to day living.
I found that each day ... I loved you more.
We've had time to explore the mind, the heart, the soul.
I rejoice in the reality I found.
Beyond my expectations, beyond my dreams ... I found you.
I no longer look back to what was or what should have been,
the remains of my girlhood dreams,
instead I look forward to new beginnings,
and each new beginning ... begins with you.
Today I am a woman grown ... who knows what a man should be,
and you are the man ... who taught me.
"Trust me," you said, and I do ... Sweetheart I love only you.
Teach me ... teach me more ... of "sweet awakening."

The Recipe

I listened to the words he spoke ... they were confusing ... contradicting,
and then I listened once again ... with my heart.
I watched his actions and his antics ... trying to separate fact and fiction,
and then I watched once again ... this time with my mind,
and that was good ... for now I fully understood.
I took the words he spoke and mixed them with the actions and reactions.
I added in his past and just a dash of the passion ... I had glimpsed.
I took the doubt and sifted it out,
as I remembered the love, laughter, peace,
and released those also into the potion,
getting the sweet fragrance of our emotion.
I added just a twist of my own pain to lessen his pain,
and from the memories I held in my heart ... of his dear heart,
only one thing remained.
I took my faith and strength and bound it all together,
shaking it up,
and when the recipe blended ... I could not doubt,
that love ... was what our relationship ... was all about.
I took a dash of sincerity and threw in a large wedge of truth,
and the power of the two combined ... invaded my mind.
I took the man that could not see and placed in his arms,
the woman ... too easily deceived,
and made them believe ... in the recipe.

WINDOW VIEWS

The Dictates of Society

All day long I sit here doing my work and keeping an eye to the picture before me, enchanting, ever-changing and entertaining. As people come upon my window which reflects like a mirror, I watch amused to see what they will do. They invariably do something, checking out the perfection of self. They see only the reflection of themselves while I notice their reaction to the self that they see. My window beckons young and old and one by one they come.

Is it vanity, curiosity, insecurity? Mothers with children running at their feet pause and quickly take a peek. They smile or frown then turn away. I have had ties straightened, skirts adjusted, hips swaying or swaggering, hair flipped. This is not vanity and no mystery and as basic and human as we all can be. I sit quietly and enjoy the view. Would not you?

Do the **dictates of society** and the standards of perfection that they set, present us with insecurities that can't be met? Are these insecurities so immense that we require physical proof of our right to acceptance by a world based **largely on shallow**? Are those of us blessed with passable physical beauty, grateful for that blessing? Are we even aware that it is one?

I wonder how those less fortunate, the not fair of face, the ragamuffins, the illiterate, you get the picture, how can they stand up and face the **self-appointed judges of society** who have displaced self-worth?

Ask yourself if you and I who can safely pass the critical eyes of our self centered and shallow world need the reassurance of the looking glass, how do those not so blessed achieve acceptance? Would you and I survive with the odds stacked against us? Would we have the **strength of character** even to begin ... with less than the perfection ... we have been given? Perhaps during the course of our too busy lives, we should take the time to reflect on all the souls that we neglect! Ask yourself if we steer away from the **imperfect**, the **impoverished**, the **derelict**?

Do we frown upon or pass judgement on the babies who are having babies, or stiletto heels and tight little skirts or the ragged old man who hangs out in the park, a brown bag not quite hidden in his threadbare shirt? Do we find ourselves criticizing the frequenters of the doughnut shops who look like they do not need that doughnut?

Snap judgements are part and parcel of our society and yet we do not look any deeper to discover the history of those we would condemn. In smug satisfaction we proudly hold up our head. Faced with their lives, would we have managed better than them? Just thoughts ... just pondering.

The paddy wagon is dropping another load of humanity ... outside my window. I often wonder just what circumstance brought them here? What exactly is their story and would it make a difference if I knew?

Always more questions. **Do you have them too?** Are the thoughts we sometimes have, perhaps a form of **unintended abuse**?

The Birthing Legend
(On a Lighter Note)

There is a legend going round about that in the beginning when babies were ready to come into the world a decision abut gender, must be made. During the birthing procedure if it is a boy the delivery stops halfway. An oath is then taken by said child to be a constant source of irritation to the female sex. If they refuse ... they are immediately changed into a girl. Now this oath is necessary because there must be opposition in all things in the universe.

So throughout their lives boys bring us to anger, cause us pain, confuse us by their own confusion again and again and again. We allow that for despite that ... they are loveable. And so I begin to understand the complexities of the very human, often little boy, modern man.

Try as he will, he needs our direction, our understanding, our support and our love. My gut feelings say not to ignore this deep tenderness that I feel, and to acknowledge the desire to protect and to initiate laughter and bring joy. My gut feelings say you need me, you sweet, misguided and very stubborn man. To save you from yourself the selfless thing to do is ... hold on. You see the other side of the legend reads, "and a baby girl was born" and she smiled and the world smiled with her and when she started to talk, she kept on talking until people listened and she cared at an early age for her dolls and her kittens and her brothers ... she "mothered."

Now the baby girl wasn't perfect. She often hugged her kittens too tight and her dolls were bathed with heads under water giving her brothers a fright. But she was loved in spite of her imperfections!

The baby girl and the baby boy were as different from each other as night to day but they complimented each other in the most extraordinary way. It was like a missing piece in a favourite puzzle ... when joined together ... they fit like no other.

The baby boy was you and the baby girl was me and it is DESTINY. The ending no matter how many times you read it is the same, for legends cannot change and stories are written to entertain and I hope you have been.

To My Sons

Have I told you lately that "**I love you.**" That I am proud of you. Always was and always will be. I understand that your heart is good. I know that you are strong. I believe in you, in your thoughts and your actions and your feelings.

Search for and find your own truth my sons. Dare to dream your own dreams. Reach beyond the stars for the sun and the moon and the sky. I know you can do this if you but try.

As the hand of time slowly closes about this heart of mine ... I know that I can leave the future up to you both. Your life is yours to choose. I pray only that you will walk under the protection of God's love ... lead with your heart and follow through ... believe in self every day of your life.

Life is such a fragile thing. It's like hanging on a tiny string that could drift away tomorrow and be lost forever in the wind. Make each second count. Mark each minute as special, each hour as a gift and each day as an accomplishment.

Live life with sunshine in your soul and a song in your heart. Remember always the beauty of you and search forever for "**clarity in truth.**"

Bullying and Control

Hello again. Have you ever found yourself in the wrong place at the wrong time and with the wrong people? I was coming out of a store in the plaza. It was mild for December and rain was falling softly in the near darkness as I headed towards my little sunfire. The parking lot was nearly empty at the supper hour. I was parked six spots down from the store and a pickup truck had just left ahead of me. I watched as he went into the turn to leave and saw his back break lights flash on. I automatically stopped but the truck didn't he rammed the gears into reverse without checking and started backing up.

There was no time to reverse my car and no space to get out of his way. There was a car to the left of me waiting for me to move. The trucker didn't hear my horn blasting or if he did ... he did not care. His back end with trailer hitch lifted my front bumper off the ground. It all happened so quickly and I had not moved an inch. Stunned and then angry I moved to get out of my car. The stranger waved me back in. Stubbornly I refused as I looked at the damage. I noticed someone striding towards me. It was a well-dressed older man and as he moved closer he started yelling at me. Why? I don't know. "Lady you have to watch what you are doing ... you were driving way too close." Dumbfounded my mouth dropped open, my eyes popped and I stared at this complete stranger as if he were some kind of lunatic. "**What?**" I stammered, sure that I must have heard incorrectly. He said, "I saw the whole thing and you were driving too close." This was getting pretty bizarre. Gaining some courage I said, "wait a minute. If you saw the whole thing then you know that is not what just happened here. Why are you lying?"

At this point I felt a shadow coming in from my right and there I was in a darkened, rainy parking lot sandwiched between two large and threatening strangers. In total disbelief as to what was happening, I turned and demanded in a near hysterical voice, of the man who had just smashed my vehicle, "tell him what happened." I would like to make it perfectly clear that I am not in the habit of shouting at anyone. I was clearly losing it. We waited for his reply. "I don't know. You must have been travelling too close." Hello! Could this farce really be happening. Frantically I found myself scanning the parking lot for an ally, someone who didn't need glasses. They had all gone.

It took only a few seconds to ascertain that no help would be coming. I was shaking from reaction as well as the rain. I am five foot three and both of these men, (dare I call them that) were the same height, six feet easily and hefty beef and beer lovers, weighing in at close to two hundred pounds.

Both men were in their early sixties and the witness was a well-dressed man driving a new model, mustard yellow suburban. The trucker was a ragamuffin with ill fitting jean overalls and a down in the mouth look as if he had seen better times. I was feeling a little sorry for me. Looking from one to the other, a light dawned as if all the lights in the parking lot grew brighter and I very calmly said, "wait a minute, this all makes perfect sense, you two are friends." There was a short, charged Silence as they communicated silently over my head and then of course ... they denied it. It was clear as day to me.

My panic subsided. I was no longer confused. I had them. The witness slid like the snake he was back into his car, without another word to me. He was gone before I could write down his plate number. For the record the trucker was sporting no plates on front or back and he had no insurance with him. That itself was a story. For all I knew it could have been stolen.

This was a pure case of bullying. It is done by those without backbone. They have absolutely nothing to recommend them and so wander through life beating up physically or emotionally those who need protection. It makes them feel powerful. Bullies are mean, small minded, without conscience or ethics and most certainly **without honour**. They come in all shapes, sizes, ages and can be very dangerous. **They attack like savage dogs** out of control to make us feel ... out of control.

Driving home I wondered if perhaps this was some kind of a scam for defenseless women alone at night. The trucker followed me home right into my parking lot. It was the main reason for contacting the police. It had me scared. He now knew where I lived. Intimidation. I stayed in my car with the doors locked till he left. He did not know which apartment was mine.

If it wasn't to save a dollar then I wonder what all that mess was really about. The ironic part is that I would have settled for an apology. It would have been so easy for him to say "sorry." I am sorry he didn't ... not for me but for him. How very dreadful it must be to live a life ... devoid of common decency. It might be interesting to know that this poor downtrodden man lives in a mansion in North Oshawa with a triple garage and could well afford to fix the damage. Yes of course I followed through. What else could I do? I needed to know.

So my friend, if a bully walks into your world ... refuse to play along. Stand up to them and call their bluff or simply with dignity walk away. None of them are worthy of your time. Those needing power and control need to be ... **controlled**, but it is not our job. Be aware. Be ready. Be safe. Bullies are only bits of fluff scattered in the wind.

Natures Bounty

Here I am at work. My mornings here are slow and my thoughts are allowed to wander aimlessly, dependant on my mood. My eyes wander too, peering through my window to an ever changing and colourful view. **Thought and vision often intertwine**. I have time.

The heat hangs heavy, a thick haze pressing down gently, against the dewdrops that lay glistening in the grass, drying them intact where they sit ... like tiny teardrops caught in glass.

The temperature is palatable only by the presence of a soft summer breeze that skips and flirts through the flower beds turning colourful heads with its passage. The friendly breeze swiftly lifts and swirls high to tickle the underbelly of trapped leaves ... stirring them to a giggling, chattering rustle. The impish breeze catches and carries their whispering on the joyful current of the wind.

Sunlight washes the landscape with an artists hand in rays of silver and white. Birds on winged flight race across the sky to dip ... to dive. A great white gull spreads its powerful wings, soaring high and angles into the sky to disappear from view in a cloud of white.

Crows with their distinctive "caw, caw' disturb the morning stillness as they land in the giant oak. A tiny brown wren walks boldly on hot pavement into a sun heated puddle and dipping his wing tips into natures bath, he thrashes about.

A few cars are parking in the cracked lot and my day is about to begin. Anything can happen and usually does. **The beauty outside my window lingers in my mind**. Satisfied I'm ready to begin my day.

I will let you go for now to begin your own day. Do it your own way.

Life's Confusion

Hello, Good Morning. How are you feeling? A little tired? Me too. It's lonely at 3:00 am. I am getting a little too old for this. I was busy sitting in front of the TV and watching Home and Garden. It goes on for hours. The ideas are wonderful but I have no energy even to begin. Anyway it is nice to know that I am not the only one awake.

There is a slow stream of traffic humming along on wet streets, under foggy street-lamps, beneath a sliver of moon. The magnificent tree outside my window is stretching its branches in the warm damp air. I can see buds sprouting, showing as a lighter shade of dark in this early morning light. Tim's still has a car or two, so I know that you are out there ... awake in my corner of the world.

My home is a wreck for I am hardly ever here and then just long enough to run in and make a mess. I look around not knowing where to begin and so I don't ... begin that is. I procrastinate. It has become one of my favourite pastimes. Just kidding. I believe it is giving me nightmares. Just as soon as my head touches the pillow ... no matter how exhausted I am, my mind wakes up counting the many things I have yet to do. What about you?

Have you ever felt like you were running around like a chicken with its head off, travelling down countless highways, taking annoying side trips? Are you sometimes too rushed to feel anything but lost? What is that all about anyway? Do you have any idea? I get in my car and immediately, if not sooner, find myself in the middle of a traffic jam. Who needs that? If I even try to go the speed limit everyone around me would be angry ... so of course I speed right along with them. Even so I am usually five minutes late for work every single day. How does this happen? No really ... my boss would like an answer. I'm all out of excuses.

I'm working on 3 to 4 hours sleep so I am looking as wrecked as my house. I've been told I'm pretty scary. Bright light ... there is after all an advantage for poor eyesight. I'm not into pettiness, gossip, control and I've never been able to keep up with the Jones' (who are they anyway?) so I usually take a short cut to get ahead, just for fun or smile as they pass me in the fast lane. I guess it's a matter of perspective.

What really goes on in the hearts and minds of those around us? Why do we do what we do? What is it that you are thinking right now and in the course of my day will that impact on me, on you, on us? The question **WHY** is important. **Let's hold onto this truth**.

My computer is shouting the time as 5:18 am. The traffic is humming along nicely now on its way to somewhere and these ancient bones need to rest. I have enjoyed our journey together. Perhaps we will meet again some time or perhaps not. Until then slow down, we matter. No matter what.

The Perfect House

Hello. Its been a while since last we spoke. Longer since I put fingers to keys and let my thoughts wander. Today I was invited by friends to visit a strangers home undergoing major renovations. The perfect house? In an area where the construction of new homes has become our major industry and rooftops with chimneys are covering up our precious fertile fields, where the rabbit, the fox and the deer are being pushed back and displaced with total disregard and nature beckoning is but a memory of a time when we had time ... to be beckoned, is there room for such a thing as the perfect house and to whom would it be perfect ... if it could be found?

This treasure, this find, this perfect house was set back from a busy street and nestled into a small woods. It was spring and you could hear the rushing of the creek not 30 feet from the back door. There was a heavy, solid door on huge hinges set into the front entrance. The facing wall held hand planted sharp and shiny stones and was to be kept as original, but the door was to be replaced by modern. The floors had been taken down to wood planking and laid at an angle leaving only plain, solid, sweet smelling wood. Walking around the corner we entered a huge dining room with drywall partitions spaced two feet apart down its entire length and giving a clear view to the sunken living room with cozy corner fireplace and a wall of floor to ceiling windows looking into the back garden. It was evening but the feeling was one of light, air, space.

The kitchen stood in a state of disarray with cupboards freshly painted sitting on an open plank floor. Kitchen tiles were in heavy boxes leaning into a deserted corner and blank areas gaped openly waiting for the new appliances to come. It was a compact open concept area except for a short wall where a pass-through window was to be inserted.

The back wall of the house facing the kitchen had a door that led outside to a long and wide deck. I stepped out into the darkness and was enveloped by the slippery breeze, the rushing creek and the shadowy shape of trees and plants. The busy street out front was forgotten. For those few moments I was lost in the beauty of the garden.

Our guide explained the absence of things no longer there. The circular stairs to the basement, gone. The dark wood walls of panelling replaced by fresh drywall. Curved archways were now square. The rocks and water fountain had been replaced by nothing but useable space. Drywall dust lay thick upon the open floor boards and landed gently on the walls, it covered the ledges and tinted the windows. We walked around pails and ladders ... the contrast between finished and yet to do, refreshing, exciting, as this unique place was turned into someone else's dream. The possibilities lay scattered all about me and I marvelled at what it could be.

I had not realized that our tour had just begun. There was a whole other thing happening below ground and that turned out to be the most perfect. We carefully stepped down, stairs too steep and too narrow for this old girl. With our feet planted on unfinished floor, we made our way down a hall and turned the corner. It was there that for me the journey ended. We stood on one of those new cushioned subfloors. The room itself was not very large ... a kitchen under construction. Second-hand cupboards were off to the right, incomplete but with a new boxed in light secured proudly over the sink. Off to the left was a dividing wall where the kitchen flanked the bedroom and in its center was an ancient wooden door and on either side of this, as raw and beautiful as age can make them were two original paned windows, complete with peeling green paint, framed by the back side of the rough wooden panelling that had been ripped off the walls upstairs. Ingenious ... delightfully appealing ... and why ever not.

I so much needed my camera for I know that words will never fully capture the picture that lingers in my mind and the beauty that I found there in that unfinished room. In the very centre of that tiny basement room stood a simple, narrow wooden table facing me lengthwise. It was covered with some tools ... a tape measure ... a shiny new country home decorating book and an unfinished plate of food. At the head of the table, not sanctioning our intrusion, not condemning, not caring ... sat a man. He was facing me with work-boots planted firmly on the subfloor, forearms resting solidly on either side of his late-night dinner. He was silent and still with watchful eyes.

He was covered in construction dust. It lay heavy upon his powerful shoulders. It weighed down his hair, changing its colour from brown to off white grey. The stubble of his face caught the dust gently in passing and the sleeves of his steel blue ribbed sweater were shoved carelessly up to his elbows leaving the lean muscles of his forearms exposed. The fine hair there smeared thick with dust and sparkling in the light from a single bald ceiling bulb. He was bone weary, exhausted, starving and yet totally focused on, his world ... his schedule ... his creation. This man would not or could not tear himself away from his current project. He was a dreamer, an artist and a finisher and that tiny space was filled with his determination ... sparkling with his ideas.

We were shown into a huge unfinished part of the basement with a cold cement floor. This was to be the living room. For the record this home did not originally have a walk-out basement. The earth had pressed solid and damp and inch upon inch against the outside wall. The man we had left diving into his dinner had simply dug out the heavy wet soil creating a large open area of light and space where once the earth had stood. He hewed out the shape of the steps leading up and out, cut into the earth wide and long. Into the newly exposed cement wall he cut and placed a large patio door. I cannot even begin to imagine taking on such a monumental task.

I have no doubt that the finished product will be perfect. The dedication, quality, artistic originality and strength of this one simple man renews my faith in the countless possibilities that surround us, if only we had the vision to see. It's exciting and humbling to stand in the presence of such excellence.

As to the perfect house, any hovel can be a home if lovingly tended by its owner. This house is loved.

A Ball of Yarn

Life is one wonderous, unexpected, beautiful and sometime scary adventures that we were meant to discover. It has so many factions that we as mere mortals may not have enough time to explore to our hearts content. Time does matter.

Sometimes life is like a ball of coloured yarn, unravelling. You might ask how could this be when normally yarn is formed into a set pattern done with loving hands. I ask you to trust your imagination.

A playful kitten pounces upon the unsuspecting ball of yarn. As the ball falls to the floor the kitten follows. He stalks his prey and nudges it with his tiny nose. The coloured ball begins to roll. A furry paw swipes at it and the ball starts to unravel. It travels under couches, over slippers, around corners. It spins out of sight. On padded feet the kitten creeps. He discovers it once more as he slides on the kitchen floor. Playfully the kitten swats again and off the ball rolls. The ball is smaller now, its colours dim and finally it disappears leaving behind but a trail of string.

The journey has been exciting, unexpected, not planned, spontaneous. Life is like that. This ball of yarn was not forced into a "set pattern" by a "masters hand." It was allowed to run free as we ourselves were meant to be. How else would we learn and grow if not once were we allowed to explore the great unknown ... on our own.

There is a place always for the "masters hand," but part of "his" plan is that we push the borders of our world and allow our minds to self discipline and expand. Think of the possibilities!

They are limitless.

The Mystery of Us

There is a reason for this journey. There are nuggets of gold to be found on every pathway we follow and answers to all our questions from every person that we allow into our inner circle. They will in some way **enhance the quality** of our life.

Never doubt that there is much that we can learn from one another. Everything that we experience, adds dimension to our life, shines light upon new horizons. We begin to set up borders that are acceptable to us and we **walk away** from actions not conducive to our health and happiness. Every step taken brings us closer to the "**reality of self**."

Wisdom is what we have gained.

I state again, there is a purpose for this journey. I cannot stress this enough. Nothing we experience on **life's roller coaster** ... is ever lost. Believe this. We unknowingly file it away to be used for "**future reference.**"

For every person we connect with, for every path we follow, for every decision made and every mistake we make ... we learn, we grow, we become more confident. Each experience will be reflected in our future actions as we filter in, "**knowledge gained**." We should never negate anyone or anything that impacts upon our lives ... good or bad.

So ask yourself this question ... should we be building walls to surround us, to hide safe within their shadows? It is possible that we would stagnate there. Should we be climbing every mountain there is to climb with our friend "**Courage**' at our side? Which answer will lead to a life worthwhile and well lived?

Imagine now ... that life as yours. Pretty incredible ... isn't it?

Rejoice, be unafraid, there are really no mistakes we can make that cannot turn into **stumbling blocks of learning**. With each step we come closer to our "**hearts desire**" and incredibly ... our hearts desire can change with each lesson learned.

How we unravel the "**mystery of us**" is our reward. You should find at the end of the journey, that what makes you **happy** hopefully ... **is you**. You will have discovered your own

"sweet truth."

The Prisoners Cage

Hi it's me. It seems like forever since last we spoke. I've been busy, you know with life. It's a complex situation at the best of times. How are you? Really I'd like to know. Surviving the course I hope. When you think of it, sometimes hope is the only answer left to us.

The sun is hot and strong for an end of September day. The leaves are just beginning to dress in a multitude of glorious colours. After nearly five years my "**window view**" is partially blocked and I am not happy about that. I am still in front of my large office window with the double paned glass and the one-way view. I am looking out at my world, looking out at you but now to the right, drills are drilling, saws are eating metal, power supplies are humming and dusty dirt covered men are swarming in and around a large 25 x 35 foot wired pen that is sitting in the middle of my parking lot. The noise is obscene. **The birds have flown the coop**. Inside our spirits droop as this monstrosity comes together. It is a holding tank for the "**prisoner carrying paddy wagons**," bringing their cargo to the courts upstairs.

This construction will be permanently blocking more than half my view of the tiny meadow with its swamp grasses swaying in harmony with the breeze. It is playing havoc with the beautiful edging of trees which surround the hilltop cemetery. Things will never be quite the same. There is ever and constantly change and I do not roll with it as sweetly as once I did. Now there will be no you ... for me to talk to or at least very few. You can no longer stroll casually past my window. Now you will be walking out and around this absurd contraption that confines bodies and limits minds ... destroying by its mere presence ... dreams. I may as well retire my pen ... for who then is there left to communicate with.

Shovels scrape against the pavement picking up smashed bits of concrete, sawdust chips, cut metal. Scaffolding sits directly in my line of vision ... pressed tight against my window. Welding tools shoot sprays of firelight into the air as heat hits metal and melts.

This building is without beauty. There are no sweeping lines or sun catching windows. There are no windows and the large double swing doors are locked tight against the possibility of flight. A motor just started up again. The time is 2:45 pm. The gloves are going on and the face masks slip into place. Amidst a tangle of extension cords ... safety booted feet move to the last line of unfinished wire mesh and sparks start to fly. The rat a tat tat of the gun makes its own rhythm of music and blue and white light mixes with golden sparks. The light is beautiful but the smoke from burnt metal quickly disperses that beauty. An extension ladder falls heavily on the inside wall and clangs into its needed height. Noise and confusion continue.

It appears that for now my quiet times for reflection are gone. Surely time will reveal some good and as yet, not understood value to this bizarre cage growing inch by inch, more ugly before my eyes. I was not ready for this change nor is it wanted. I was not consulted and why should I be? I am but one soul searching Heaven in a world that is racing to Hell ... or sometimes it seems that way. I actually enjoy our daily visitors ... the prisoners, with their different faces and cocky attitudes. Their fashion parade of bright orange, standard issue, statement making uniforms, fitting differently on each one. I shall miss the cigarette butt chasing, the leg shackle shuffle and the step up and hop door entry. Engaging grins and mischievous eyes mix with cold looks and harsh rough faces. Ever changing are the faces and the personalities ... the size and shapes and the colours of our guests. The questions that went unanswered in our minds as to what they had done, why they were there and where they were going ... literally, figuratively, hopefully, all this will be lost to me now and therefore I too will lose.

The tap tap of the funky hammer echoes sharply in the now still air. The work trucks have all gone save only one. The day melts into the late afternoon sun as I sit ... wilting in depression.

I look up to see the cold metal doors swing open to admit its first paddy wagon. It comes lumbering in through the wide double doors to wait in this man-made tomb to pick up the remains of humanity from their day in court. In single file they come chained together one by one, their feet hobbled, their gaze riveted upon the wires of yet another cage. I see them now only with blurred vision as the diamond mesh fence imprints shadows upon their features. When the final walls go up and darkness falls upon this man-made cave ... I will see them no more. Now men restrained by the laws that contain them are walking in shadow, hidden, perhaps more ... safe? They are ghosts without faces, without form, without voice.

At the end of this long day I begin to see of what use the wire cage is to me. Once my window view, was free of all boundaries. I was surrounded only with natures miracles, limitless vistas and endless sky. The ugliness of the box on my perimeter is a constant reminder of limitations, those of society but more important those that we as mere humans inflict upon ourselves. There is no cage built by man that can contain the humans soul. No Army so strong that the mind it can destroy. No wall so high that a heart cannot soar, except those that we ourselves build or invent. Freedom remains here, safe within, if we allow it to be so. We either make or destroy this "gift of life." The choices, they are ours.

I am old and still I dream. Somehow I still believe ... unbelievably in me. Deep inside where no one else can see, I remain always who I am, allowing nobody and nothing to strip me of my identity. For all the many tragedies mixed with joys that each of us carries, we must remember to love us best. Accept not the dictates of others, their attacks upon our rights and our abilities. Even those closest to our hearts have no real understanding of the hearts we have given them to hold. Eventually we will come to understand and accept this simple fact. We meet as travellers on this road called life yet each of us ultimately travels alone with the few possession we will ever truly own ... **our heart ... our mind ... our soul**.

I guess I got to rambling, wandering amok amongst the corridors of my mind. Know you are not forgotten. Each one of us will make a difference ... a contribution to this "Gift of Life." And What that will be ... is entirely up to us. Perhaps we will meet again within the Region of my Window View. Know it would be nothing ... without you.

The Phone Call

Light turns to darkest night and finds them tangled beneath the covers, tangled in each others' arms with their bodies warm and spent in exhausted sleep ... complete ... and at peace. His arm hugs her slender waist fitting her instinctively in place against his broad chest ... her head coming to rest just beneath his chin ... her hand in his.

Their awareness of one another never ends. If he turns she snuggles closer in ... fitting in perfect harmony ... continuous motion, explosive, complete, when two hearts in tune meet. Like a ballet performed effortlessly ... their need for each other does not cease. Together they hold the world at bay.

Their breathing becomes erratic. From sleep to wakefulness, simultaneous, unaware of the transition ... passion and love forge them together once again, moving in rhythm, insatiable with the need to feed one another. Like a flower in bloom her scent fills the room. She opens up ... he enters in ... love envelopes them.

Somewhere between forgetfulness and awakening ... his hand stretches for the phone. It rings and with sleep filled voice his love sweetly answers him. "Goodmorning ... I love you. I dreamed I was in your arms all night long." He replies, "you were and I love you too. Sweetheart I miss you."

His thoughts still tangled in his dreams ... his dreams become reality it seems. Time and distance cannot erase the power of two hearts in place. Love brings them together always in one special place. Happy ... safe.

Unexpected Blessings

Hello again. Good Morning. Are you out there somewhere in my world? I woke today thinking thoughts of you ... those I have yet to meet. It has been far too long since we connected through the windows of my mind. It seems like years since I put pen to paper or as we say now ... fingers to keys. It has been far too long since I allowed my thoughts to wander down the corridors of my mind. The journey today started with you. Perhaps you think that strange.

I woke to the constant sounds of tires hitting pavement ... the sounds mixed with fallen drops of rain squished ... displaced between hot treaded tires. The sounds are pleasant, familiar, soothing ... the rhythm constant. I cannot hear the birds. They must be sleeping snug in their nests and waiting for the air to be less heavy. There is no blue sky, no fluffy clouds of white, no sun.

Sheets of dampened mist fly by my window ... millions upon millions of tiny perfect drops in vertical invisible lines race to feed the hungry earth below.

The view from my window is taken up fully with one magnificent tree, many branched with wide and sturdy trunk and leaves of deepest green. Its beauty ... humbles me as does the miracle ... God given that allows me to see. **I take nothing for granted**. If life has taught me anything ... it has taught me that. **There are no guarantees**. We have but today, this hour, this minute ... to choose happy.

With only the faith that has always sustained me. I embrace this moment and the "**gift of life**" I have been given. "**It is enough!**"

Marsh Hill Road

It was late spring 2003, with summer edging the horizon. The sun was shining, the breeze warm and tires were eating up the pavement. Time slipped away as we zigged and zagged from the Purple Woods, westward and north. We followed the sunshine up hills and down into forested valleys, enchanted with the world outside our windows.

Seven minutes out of Manchester, with countless miles and many snapped pictures behind us we turned west once again. I don't know why. We ended at the corner of Marsh Hill Road and the car stopped on the top of a hill connected by farms with a beautiful view. Just in front of us, catching us off balance, sitting majestic in the sunlight but strangely silent was a mansion. It was oddly displaced among the country landscape.

All the bottom windows were boarded up with blue ... the wood warm against the red brick. Quite frankly it captured our attention ... fired our imagination. Questions without answers swirled in our heads. There were no people, no sign of habitation, no breath of life.

Throughout the day we had stopped to snap pictures of ducks on ponds and small barnyard baby goats behind a wooden rail fence. There was an old farmhouse with range chickens wandering at will over the front garden. We captured two horses leaning into an ancient little truck filled with sweet smelling hay and we snapped pictures of the mansion from many angles.

I wove dreams around that mansion. It would creep into my thoughts at unexpected moments when time allowed thoughts to wander. We went for many drives in countless directions as summer exploded and nature beckoned. We came a second time by choice ... to the mansion. Was anybody there now or had it just been closed for the winter? Was it as beautiful as we remembered? It stood exactly as in memory, a house but not a home.

The door needed to be open, and the windows raised for the breezes to play up the stairs. The sun waited to warm the walls and chase the shadows away. It needed voices and gardens and window boxes full of colour and curtains crisp ... rippling in the wind. It needed to breathe.

It seemed a shame to us to see such a wasted house, cold, lifeless, slowly rotting away with neglect. Our questions remained unanswered and we foolishly followed through with a letter to the owner. It was answered indirectly. The property is now under security with signs on the gate and a car in the drive. It no longer stands alone, yet it remains unloved, not a home ... just a dream lost now and forgotten.

Forever Changes

Hello, an early Good Morning. Are you out there awake somewhere in my world? I settled down just before midnight, exhausted from a busy day and all that. As soon as I did my mind came awake and thoughts ... not sleep related started tumbling over one another in an effort to be heard. What is all that about?

I scrunched my eyes more firmly shut and tried to block the sound of cars humming along the road outside my window. It's never really dark in here. Even with the blinds closed the street-lights push against the window-pane and slide silently through the blind to bounce off the mirror across the room.

I lay patiently waiting for blessed sleep to release me from this day. It's not happening. It's hopeless.

I slip out of bed and wander down the hall searching for a clock with the correct time. The world sprang forward leaving me one hour behind. The time is 2:18 am and I have wasted two hours of precious time in total exasperation. Here I am once again sitting in front of my computer and putting fingers to keys and talking to you and whoever may be sleepless and listening. I find that there are few minutes in the frenzy of our days for rational thought. It seems that late at night or dawns awakening are the only time I have for myself and so here I am.

We just had a major shake up at work. I along with others were happily minding our own business when somebody gave us a push in a direction we didn't want to go. We fought them with righteous indignation ... laying reason on the table. The changes still took place. We are now waiting for the dust to settle and curious to see where the last domino will fall and when.

There are few smiling faces at this moment and those not yet displaced are sitting quietly, fading into the desktops with lowered voices and lower heads. They anxiously wait for the axe to fall, hoping not to be noticed at all. I hope someone is happy somewhere and wonder about the motivation behind such an upheaval. Anyhow it no longer matters. I've settled into my new location and my eyes are feasting on different faces. The challenges are waking up all my survival instincts so I think I will be happy with this move. To be or not to be happy ... that is the question. As always there is but one choice for me. Regardless, I refuse to be beaten, broken, destroyed and so I will valiantly fight back until I have this new position firmly under control.

It is in our nature to fight against that which we do not know. It's called survival and it is mixed up somehow with fear. This is good ... a wake up call ... to stretch our imaginations and embrace countless opportunities that beckon and so this morning at 3:06 am you find me smiling. As usual my thoughts moved me to where I needed to go. They were weighing on my mind. Perhaps now sleep will claim me. The journey continues, made sweeter by those we meet along the way. It's a new day, an adventure. It's called life and I am grateful to be here ... to live it.

The Right to be Unique

God made each one of us as a unique entity. There is no one anywhere exactly like us. We should rejoice in this fact. We each react if only fractionally, a tad differently, to the same outside interactions. I might **hear a bird song at dawn** and find it **beautiful** and you might **throw a pillow over your head** to drown out what you perceive as **noise**.

When I was young I was told that we need contrasts in all things or they would be of no value to us. They would hold no meaning. How would we differentiate between good and evil if we had no experience of one of these elements? How does water feel as compared to air? We appreciate warmth and relate it to summer because if you live here the winters are brutally cold. Of course I have friends that prefer the cold. I don't get it and yet though we differ in thoughts, minds, hearts at times, we are still the best of friends.

I might look frumpy in mismatched colours and styles that I love and you might be perfectly put together in designer duds. I respect your right to be happy with your choices and usually I am happy in mine. We can all learn from each other or at least we should try. The world minute by minute is becoming so much smaller than ever before. Countries that we many never have heard of could be knocking at our door. Are we going to be ready for this? Will the world be able to adjust to our differences and live in harmony with one another? This is a huge question. Somewhere there is an answer. We must believe in this.

With faith I walk these roads down below trying to hold onto a sense of self. I will never be perfect but I will remain ... **perfect in my imperfections**. The wonders of the world surround me. Know that you are one of those wonders. By your mere existence, by what you do and what you accomplish ... you will impact my world.

We all matter ... no matter what. Never forget that. Embrace every single moment to give you strength to embrace the next. The journey that you make and how you make it, is what should be important to you. **Who am I really?** The answer to that question will bring **clarity** to our life and with wonder ... we will continue this journey.

Remember each one of us is ... unique ... individual ... precious.

Passages of Time

Hello again. Are you awake yet? The time is 6:15 am. The apartment is chilly. Night has given way to mornings first light. The street outside my window has its first stirrings of wheels, swishing on wet pavement. The plaza across the street is still asleep. Perhaps you are too.

I have made my way to the living room and stand amidst the clutter I have accumulated that has made this place a home to me. Every where I look I see memories. I switch on minimal lights, just enough to see. The room is subdued.

My corner garden chair is stuffed with grasses and silver dollars with ducks and small birds hidden within the tiny branches. It is backed by a Chinese screen and a colourful oriental umbrella. I love that corner of this large square room.

An antique fireplace screen is fanned out like the tail of a peacock in brass and is filtering light in patterns across the hardwood floor. I like it.

A tiny wooden rocking horse sits silently in the shadows of this fragile light. He seems at home there in that particular spot. When my granddaughter, Cassie comes over, she climbs upon his back and rocks rapidly, back and forth, her tiny hands tight, her eyes alight with joy.

The clock on the shelf beats a steady ticking rhythm to mark the passage of time. I pick up my pen or in modern times put fingers to keys as thoughts and feelings and memories clamour for clarity.

I have found peace here in this corner of the world. I'm safe in this place that surrounds me with loving memories. Hope abides within my heart and holds me steadily on my journey to almost anywhere I wish to go. I have choices.

Time has jumped ahead and a new day awaits and I must hurry to get ready for work. I embrace my ability to do so. **I actually love my job. What a gift that is!** Have a good day. Choose your own way and remember to be happy. Until next time ... and time is a factor... unpredictable as that seems.

Building Character

There are defining moments not quite forgotten in our past that have shaped and molded us. Moments that have set us on paths that we may never have taken. Moments that have vibrated us into an awareness in millions of small and vital ways.

I know that together, bit by bit they shaped and defined my life as step by step I stretched into my world. These lasting impressions blasted my mind into thoughts that mattered and ways of thinking and analyzing how my world worked and my reactions to the world.

With each step taken from our earliest memories and every lesson learned, we have been building "**our chatacter**." We are ready and able to face any given situation that may befall us. We are strong, we have spent a lifetime building blocks upon which to stand, strong and sure and near perfect. This is our "**solid foundation**."

This will give us food for the soul and thoughts ... to free our minds.

One of the most important lessons I learned as a very young teen happened at a youth conference in Toronto. Drawn to and standing at the fringe of a crowd of quiet teenagers, (**that in itself not natural**) I watched a teenage boy holding them all in thrall. My very first reaction was that he was not attractive, so what exactly was the draw? Like a sponge needing an answer to the question of "**why**" I waited to learn just exactly what there was about this young boy that appeared to be so exciting to the others. As I listened to him entertain, talk, make us laugh, I totally forgot my first impressions. I no longer saw an unattractive boy, who was too tall and very skinny with a bad haircut and acne scarred face. I stood entranced watching a "**power house**" of intelligence, humour and personality, who had total confidence in who he was.

To find such strength in one so young was an inspiration to me. His "beauty" is what I saw. I was probably around thirteen and everywhere I looked there were lessons to be learned and I found that amazing. I never forgot this lesson and many years later I related this concept of beauty to my two oldest granddaughters who are truly beautiful. "**Never forget that outward beauty is a gift and it will make your life easier. Never ... abuse this gift**."

I stood rocking a little boy in my arms. He was missing his mom. Tears were running down his cheeks. I carried him to the patio door and pointing my finger I whispered, "**look**." The tears stopped as we watched rain falling on towering evergreens and pointing higher we saw the sun battling to break through the clouds. The day was all confused. Silently, together we watched fat raindrops sliding along needles, green, slippery, sharp. A single drop was caught and held, just for an instant within a sunbeam ... before it plopped to the sodden earth below.

Have you ever stood in awe and watched the sun rise into a clear morning sky as it pushes against the night. There is no stopping the earths rotation. This is "**dawn awakening**."

FOR THE YOUNG & YOUNG AT HEART

Mommy Said

The sunlight played upon the window-pane,
It landed softly upon the sleeping child.
It curled the corners of her lips,
And tugged persistently, upon her lashes.
Cassie stretched into the morning and sat up in bed.
Long blonde curls tumbled ands swirled around her head.
Throwing back the covers, she landed on the floor,
and headed straight for the bedroom door.
Then she remembered what Mommy said,
"don't you dare ... wake up your sister.
She paused but for a second, then raced down the hall,
bare feet eating up the carpet ... making no sound at all.
Perhaps Kennedy was already wide awake ... for goodness sake.
She crept ... quietly ... into the room, but Kennedy was fast asleep.
She bent her head for a closer look ... to be sure.
Her curls tickling her sisters face ... the sleeping child stirred.
"OK!" she thought, climbing onto the bottom of the bed.
"I can wait." And she sat... quietly waiting,
her fingers tickling her sisters feet.
Itsy bitsy spider came next and remembering what Mommy said,
she sang softly.
Gently ... she began to bounce upon the bed,
the bounces getting larger and larger.
The bounces got so very big,
the sleeping sister bumped her head.
"Ouch" ... Kennedy sat up wide awake,
her fist rubbing her big blue eyes.
"Cassidy ... remember what Mommy said,"
"don't wake me up!"
Smiling sweetly Cassie said, "I didn't ... are you hungry?"
Slipping off the bed and holding hands,
they raced quietly ... down the hall,
two blonde heads with curls bobbing ... feet bare,
they thumped ... quietly down the stairs,
always remembering what Mommy said.

My first childrens story
INSPIRED BY:
My granddaughters ... who bring me great joy!

Feather's in Flight

Morning sun was gently breaking into the day. The pond lay in shadows under its many branched tree. Three little friends waited, watching the sky ... waiting for their friend "Feathers" to come home again.

Suzy Squirrel with her bushy tail swishing ... Floppy Froggie clean and green with feet thumping ... and Miss Funny Bunny with nose twitching.

Where was "Feathers" their magic wooden duck? He should be home by now.

High above the branches which swayed over the pond, they heard the flutter of "wings." "Feathers" dipped and dived and circled high above them and again dipped his wings ... waving to them. He glided by and he was smiling.

"You cannot imagine all the sights I've seen," he shouted happily.

"Imagine ... blue lakes with fish jumping clear of the water. I saw horses prancing in the fields and large lazy cows with big brown eyes grazing in the grass. There were so many shades of green and so many different beautiful trees with branches swaying in the breeze."

"Piglets with curly tails were playing and rolling in the mud. "**What fun**." They were pink and then turned to brown. "**Magic**" I saw a scarecrow waving his arms with the force of the wind. His job was to scare the crows away from the corn fields. "**Crazy**."

"Feathers" circled around again, lower this time skimming the pond.

"I've travelled far and my wings grow tired. I'm so sleepy." His head dipped. My what a night I've had. It was wonderful to be free. Free to be... just me.

His wings flapped ... flapped ... flapped, as he dropped ... dropped from the sky. Looking back he winked at his friends.

"I've missed you guys." He whispered softly.

"There is always tomorrow. The magic will happen again." Whispering again as he gently landed with a quiet splash into his pond. Safe ... home again ... "Feathers" eyes slowly closed and exhausted ... he slept.

The three little friends were smiling ... excited by the promise of more magic to come. They had never been farther from home. Always within sight of the giant tree and the magic of their pond. One by one they too fell asleep to dream ... dreams of places not seen and what was yet to come.

And One More Thing

Perhaps you yourself have been told by those who love you, "I suggest that you never tell anyone else about this, they will think you are crazy." Well on the off chance that I am not crazy and the possibility that you too have had a similar experience I am ready to share.

These words are not a work of fiction but of actual happenings and authenticated by a witness ... for the experience was shared by two.

I will start at the beginning. For our fathers 80th surprise party we approached the current owners of Dads, grandfather Ike's farm in Marmora, Ontario. On our way we stopped at the graveyard and were standing on opposite sides of Ike Baileys grave. At one point I raised my head and looked across at my sister who was looking straight at me, "**I just felt**," I said, and she answered, "**a warm hug**." As witnesses by two ... at the same time ... with the same emotion.

Powerful.

Dad had spent his summers on this farm and the memories made him happy. These wonderful strangers gave us permission to bring our entire family in celebration of his 80th, a surprise from all of us. Four generations arrived on the lawn to wait for his coming, 30 in all. The current farmer and his wife actually gave Dad and Mom a tour of the old farmstead. We were led around the farm by Dad who shared with us his memories: a natural spring of water was shared. We wandered through fields filled with cows and cow plops. Those of us not fit for walking were bundled into a farm wagon for the journey. We visited the river and some of us went in to splash and play. It was a loving family memory.

Three years later our intelligent, strong, amazing father had a severe stroke. His mind was still totally intact yet he could not speak and he never regained that gift. My sister and I were retired and able to do what we could for him. It was a loving and humbling experience. Any decisions regarding his health and happiness were done by all five of his children, holding only our concerns for him as a measuring stick. One day in Church Dad had an episode and the ambulance was called. He was taken to critical care in the hospital.

Shortly after we received a call from the ward asking us to come in and take care of him. He was being stubborn and un-cooperative. Pam and I went in late that night. A room was provided for us to sleep and we took turns sitting with our father. When it was my turn, I took my book and sat quietly reading beside his bed. He was peacefully asleep with the covers up to his chin. From a deep sleep dad sat straight up and looking at the ceiling his face lit up and I heard a deep belly laugh filled with so much joy. It happened over and over again. I sat very still not wanting to disturb what was happening. We were lucky we did not lose him that night. The experience shook me. It was as if Dad was meeting after a long absence, his wife, his parents, his brother and long lost and loved friends, those that had gone on before him. It was like a **joyous homecoming** and I loved seeing him so happy.

When Pam came into the room I said, "**the strangest thing just happened.**" And I explained what had occurred. She said she knew for it had happened to her too.

Hope grew. The **journey of life** continues. I can find no other explanation, and none is necessary. Something wonderful happened to our father that night and he was overcome with **pure joy**. That we were a witness to this **private journey** of his is a **gift** we both will cherish.

Dads sister, our Aunt Wanda was very sick and we wanted to take our father to see his beloved sister one last time. He still could not speak but we found that his words were not necessary. Two of his strong young nephews left his walker downstairs and with one on each side of him, lifted Dad up that staircase. His Sister was resting in the large bed and she patted the place beside her and said, "**Kenny, come up here beside me,**" and the two of them held hands like the little children they once had been. So natural and so loving and so at peace. Happy to be together. As we stood around the bed in silence ... much moved ... Aunt Wanda, frail but with a serene happiness said to her brother, "Kenny I do not want you to grieve for me. **I have been waiting for half of my life to be reunited with my husband and I am excited to go.**"

POWERFUL!

The stillness in that room from all of us was monumental. The emotions high. The love at that moment washed over us and none of us could or would ever forget what we had witnessed. Her belief in the **next step** of her **journey** was so strong and so very beautiful. Both young and old were given a gift that day ... never to be forgotten. It was a "**gift of hope**" and an:

Everlasting journey of love ... of growth ... and of reconnecting.

It is more than enough for me, even though others may think I am crazy. I know that I am not. In a world that is roller coasting its way to a pile up of **lost souls**, perhaps **faith** and **hope** is a "**saving grace.**"

Wishes in the Wind

Into the back yard Patti ran, a chocolate cupcake in her hand.
The sun caught her golden curls and the wind blew them in a swirl.
"And what should I wish for today?" said the little girl as she played.
Stuffing the cupcake in her mouth, she jumped up and started to twirl.
Faster and faster round and round she spun. She was faster than anyone.
Then she dropped, kerplop, into grasses mixed with dandelion tops.
Step two was to close her eyes, and scrunch them tight,
then to wish with all her heart ... to make her world right.
All we saw from our window view was a little girl in periwinkle blue.
Chubby arms reached to the sky and sticky fingers tried to catch,
bits of fluff ... floating by. As we watched ...
she caught one sailing high and giggled and held on tight,
and then she made a wish ... with all her tiny might.
With eyes closed she shouted ... "I wish for a Mommy and Daddy tonight."
Patti was an orphan child ... aged five,
and she believed as little girl do,
that wishes and dreams ... can come true.
I turned to the couple beside me and they had tears in their eyes.
"This is the child ... we choose!"
"Patti ... I have a surprise for you."
She opened her eyes and looked at them and grinned a chocolate covered grin.
With the **faith of a child** she asked ... **"are you them?"**
Into the middle she sprang and each one took a little hand.
Miracles do happen ... wishes can come true.
Somewhere ... when you are ready ... there will be one for you.

Autobiography: Sheila Bailey-McLaren

To My Readers

I am from the School of Hard Knocks and Beautiful Memories.
It's "**The Human Condition**."
I write what I have Experienced, Seen, Felt, and Lived Through.
Life is everchanging filled with side roads to follow, demands to be met, and Life to be Lived. It encompasses Love, tragedy, humour, beauty.
It is a Learning Curve . If we are not learning, why are we here?
My Goal is to : Uplift, Motivate, Offer Hope, Embrace Beauty and Believe in Self.
This Hopefully leaves my Readers, with perhaps a different Perspective and the Desire to Question that which has gone before and Challenge that which is yet to come. (Clarity)
Remember always that **"You Matter."**

CPSIA information can be obtained
at www.ICGtesting.com
Printed in the USA
BVHW020302120322
631094BV00003B/13

9 781956 896992